With Worn-Out Tools

Navigating the Rituals of Midlife

D. C. LYONS

PAGE PUBLISHING, INC.
Conneaut Lake, PA

First originally published by Page Publishing 2019

ISBN 978-1-64544-123-6 (pbk)
ISBN 978-1-64544-122-9 (digital)

Printed in the United States of America

With Worn-Out Tools is dedicated to my three grandchildren, Ethan, SaNaii, and Emma. When I was on my back during the fall of 2017, you were my "ladder" back to life. When a good day was met with multiple subsequent bad days, living for you motivated me to get out of bed.

The Bible says that "a good man leaves an inheritance for his children's children." At my core, I believe that I am a good man and living long enough for me to create an "inheritance" for you three motivated me on those tough days when it took maximum effort just to rollover.

Ethan, you are "unmerited favor." I did nothing to deserve you and yet I have been enormously blessed by you being in my life. You are so smart and inquisitive. I was born for you and truly believe that you will grow to do great things

SaNaii, you are "grace personified." You are so poised, contemplative, and composed. Your wisdom defies your years and your presence is weighty although your touch is light. You will bring substance to whatever you determine to do with your time here on earth.

Emma, you are serendipity, and a lovely unexpected, sweet addition. In you, I see a streak of independence that will inspire you to be unconventional and truly unique with the heart of a rebel. Embrace all that you are and refuse to let the world define you.

You three have taught me how to give love freely and generously. You have showed me how to receive love honestly. Thank you for being my heart, my progeny, and my lifeline.

D. C. Lyons

Foreword

Courage, by definition, is strength in the face of pain or grief. As a network news producer, many of the stories I've produced over my almost twenty-year career embody some sentiment of courage. The mother who appears in front of the world to openly grieve her son while denouncing his shooting by a "good Samaritan." The actresses who outed one of Hollywood's most powerful men, so that those that come after them will hopefully never have to endure their same trials. It is courage, that strength in the face of pain and grief, that inspires these stories and the observer that connects with them.

Growing up, my cousin Darren, closer to my older sister's age than mine, was a bit of an enigma. For those of you that come from large families, you know that you may not develop the same level of closeness in relationships with all your relatives. There tends to be a closeness with some more than others, largely based on geography or parental relationships. You may see these relatives on occasion, often times joyously at weddings and then sadly at funerals. You catch up, check in on each other's general wellness, extend blessings, and then go your separate ways. But you don't really *know* these family members.

This is the type of relationship my cousin Darren and I had. From afar, I'd always observed Darren as affable. I'd also heard him sing enough to know he had natural performance talent. "Through the grapevine" I'd heard positive ramblings about his high-powered career, successes, and international travels. Things seemed really good. Until they weren't. I remember hearing about Darren's fiftieth birthday party from some cousins on Facebook. At this point of my life, Facebook is primarily a tool I use for keeping up with family, given my very busy lifestyle. I saw the pictures and he looked great, but even more, he looked happy. Darren's journey in *With Worn-Out Tools* largely begins with his birthday celebration and I can understand why. There are times in our lives where we must stand up and take notice of milestones; attention must be paid to happy moments especially when life throws us curveballs, as it always seems to. Reading about that moment and then learning about the challenges that soon followed, instantly captivated me on my initial reading.

In many ways, I was also "getting to know" my cousin through this book. I consider myself a writer and storyteller which is probably one of the hardest sentences a writer will ever write. For most writers, it doesn't matter who are you, or what you've previously written, writing is one of the most personal things you will ever do. And it can often feel overwhelming. I can't imagine what it must be like to write a memoir, to lay bare all of your hopes, dreams, *and* the not-so-glamorous parts of your personal journey. Reading *With Worn-Out Tools*, I was so impressed with the ease that Darren expressed himself. He takes the reader on the journey of his own self-discovery. Not only does this book deal with his very serious health issues that would be challenging at any point of your life, but it also explores what it's like to go through these struggles at an already-challenging point in most lives—midlife.

Navigating life is tough for all of us. Thankfully, Darren has a strong support system which he highlights in the book. While he's definitely the starring character in this memoir, his wife Elaine was there by his side, offering great support. The protagonist's hero, if you will. As Darren's cousin, it was great to see that he'd found someone who truly loved and supported him for better and worse.

So full circle moment, for me, this book accomplished many goals. I connected with a family member in a very personal way. I truly feel like I have a better understanding about who he is at the core. I learned about managing career choices, life choices, and difficult choices in general. All of which I can apply to my life. It's quite a ride Darren takes us on, weaving a tale from successful call center manager to leg amputee. Not easy. But *courage* personified. If you're reading this foreword and wondering if you should take this journey, do it. You won't regret it and you'll be better for it. I'm thankful for the opportunity to review this very intimate work and hope that everyone will enjoy it as much as I did.

Leah Smith
Emmy Award Winning News Producer
New York, New York

The Positive Self-Affirmation

I am excited by what this day will bring
I am well trained and highly motivated by the task at hand
Yesterday's problems are today's possibilities
Yesterday's obstacles are today's opportunities
I shall not fail
What I lack in skills, I will make up with enthusiasm
Victory, is my destiny, because
I am excited by what this day will bring

The Poem "If"

I was first introduced to the poem *If* by Rudyard Kipling when I was on line pledging Alpha Phi Alpha Fraternity, Inc. at George Mason University. As a nineteen-year-old music student, I enjoyed all the poems learned during that special time. The poem was motivational, though long, and it helped me to "gut through" many long nights. Years later, I would research the origin of the poem and its writer, Nobel laureate, Rudyard Kipling and the conditions under which he wrote it.

Inspired by the Scotts Born colonial adventurer Dr. Leander Starr Jameson, the poem gives advice to the path toward being a man. Not the type of hyper masculine virtues of men that we celebrate today but the virtues of manhood that are exemplified by stoic, honorable leaders; keeping your head in the midst of chaos, trusting yourself in the midst of others doubting you, risking it all - losing and not complaining; treating success and failure as equals, sitting high and looking low. All these admirable qualities are expressed in the eight schematic verses of this poem portraying the wisdom a father gives to a son on how to be an honorable man. Come to think of it, this is excellent advice for a mother to give her daughter as well! And although the characteristics of modesty and honor are rarely celebrated today, they resonated with me as a nineteen-year-old aspirant of membership in the oldest black fraternal organization for men. As I grew older these concepts continue to resonate with me. There are several powerful lines that are quoted heavily, but the line that stuck with me is the final line of the fourth stanza:

If you can bear to hear the truth you've spoken
Twisted by knaves to make a trap for fools,
Or watch the things you gave your life to, broken,
And stoop and build 'em up *with worn-out tools:*

Rebuilding with worn-out tools seems fool-hearty. Sometimes, however, you have to work the job at hand with the tools that remain. As a young man with my future in front of me I had no concept of being "worn-out." Although being overweight all my life, I had boundless energy, I was physically strong and I was stocked with a supply of confidence that defied my stature. Although weighing over 450 pounds and having grotesque bumps on the back of my head, I had the audacity to consider myself handsome, attractive, and charming. I was so big that when children were coming my way, their eyes lit up with delight as they could not believe their good fortune. They did not have to turn their heads or sneak a peek because I was coming right at them! They were not even going to get in trouble for staring or risk getting popped upside the head by their mother for being rude as I was wobbling by in plain sight. If you looked, however, beyond the layers of fat, you saw a well-groomed, immac-ulately-dressed, and good-smelling gentleman facing the world and strutting his stuff, confidently, for all the world to see. But life has a tendency to beat against your attributes, dulling them and weaken-ing them; in essence, "wearing them out." It happens to all of us! If our tools are our good looks, they wear out when those good looks begin to fade. If our tools are our physical strength and prowess, in time, we become more brittle and weak; if our tools are our charm and sharp wit, as years stack, the mind slows down and the charming comments and quips of a young man become dated and cliché. It's a coincidence that the tools wear out when you need them most. During 2017, I personally watched the things I gave my life to bro-ken: my career, broken; my home, broken; my savings, broken; and my family, broken. As a fifty-one-year-old, three major operations—a below knee amputation, a catheter placed in my chest due to kidney failure, and a stent placed in my aorta due to a 90 percent blockage in my heart—"wore out" my tools.

I have often said that my life has been a series of losing and finding myself. I lost myself when I left home and went to college. I also lost myself after the death of my dear mother. Once again, I lost myself after the ending of my first marriage. First love, first job, and leaving home are all considered the rites of passage from being a child to an adult. Theses rites have been immortalized by Hollywood celebrating new freedom and adventure through the eyes of teenaged angst. I lived long enough, however, to discover that middle age has several rites of passage as well. As you approach your mid-forties, there are similar experiences that define the third act of your life. Second marriages, career changes, grandchildren, adult children returning to live at home, health scares, and everyone you know turning fifty, just to name a few.

Our ability to navigate the losses associated with each rite determines our ultimate destiny. Will the rite forge us like fire and sharpen our tools for life after fifty, or will it deplete us of our will and energy, relegating us to go "quietly into that good night?" Whether it replenishes us or depletes us, these middle age rites of passage cannot help but shape and influence our future. After each loss, I redirected energy, discovered ways to cope, and reinvented my "bag" or my "tools" to help me find my new self. None of these life events, however, wore out my tools like the onslaught of health challenges I faced during 2017. The path back is the key. Searching for the elevator out of the basement to the top floor is the quest. Finding, grabbing, and holding on to the ladder from your setback is the "hero's journey." This is my story about the "brokenness" and the "stooping" as well as the "worn-out tools"

At the Party

My wonderful wife insisted that I have a big shindig for my fiftieth birthday. Elaine and I had met fifteen years ago in Tampa, Florida, at a conference her two daughters attended and my company cosponsored. We got married in the "Music Room" in the Plant Museum at the University of Tampa under the historic chrome domes that highlighted the downtown Tampa skyline. We had decided to be celibate until our wedding night. That was probably the reason that we met, got engaged, and married inside of nine months! We were both divorcees, so this approach led us to having long talks late into the night when we would have been otherwise engaged.

My weight made it difficult for me to stand on my feet during the entire wedding without taking a little break. I was able, however, to gather enough energy for the evening's activities. Elaine was cute in the face, thick in the waist, sweet to the touch, and well worth the wait. She really wanted to bring all my friends together to celebrate my life, and what a wonderful life it had been. A small town boy from the predominantly black town of Petersburg, Virginia, had risen to the executive ranks of several well-known organizations! Let's face it, from the shoulders of supportive parents and a lower middle-class upbringing, I had built an impressive career. Complete with an admiring network, recommendations, and accolades, career triumphs and accomplishments. I had a beautiful family with a devoted wife, two beautiful stepdaughters, and three adoring grandchildren. They were going to be my legacy. I had even maintained the love and respect of my maternal family and earned the respect of my wife's family! I was going through that phenomena that all new quinqua-genarians experience. All my friends were approaching this milestone and we were all deciding how to properly recognize the milestone! Since I normally spent my birthday in quiet reflection, I was very hesitant to take part in this type of activity. Plus, I am a counterintu-itive-type; not one for cliché activities like traditional birthday par-ties. I am the type to have a big party for a less traditional occasion. My wife, however, can be very convincing and she proudly wanted to help me celebrate a journey that had a positive impact on many lives.

I decided that if we were going to have this party, I might as well lean into the experience. I always considered myself a pretty sharp dresser with a flair for simple elegance and style. Self-indulgently, I selected the perfect outfit—a black double-breasted jacket, a black shirt, and the funkiest caramel-, rust-, and beige-checkered wool pants from Paul Fredrick of London. I had never seen anyone wear pants like this before and come to think about it, no one had ever given me a compliment while wearing them. I loved them never-theless, as they were the perfect cross between French high fashion and Morris Day-cool. Truth be told, I would have worn a fedora, a cape, and carried a walking cane on that night had I thought about it. Several months prior, I had purchased the sweetest ride I had ever owned: a 2012 black BMW 528i. As I climbed in to take the twen-ty-five-minute drive from my home to the hotel to meet my family at the venue, I thought, *What would be the best song to serve as the theme music to kick off my night? Ah yes, "Cool" by The Time.* "I'm so cool, honey/ Baby can't you see?/ Girl, I'm so cool/ ain't nobody bad like me?/ C-O-O-L/ what's that spell? C-O-O-L!"

My brother, father, and several of my close family members trav-eled the 1,200 miles from my hometown to Oklahoma City. There was my sister-in-law, my cousins, Pat and Karen, my stepmom, and my uncle with his daughter who drove in from Nebraska and Fort Worth. As I entered the banquet room at the newly renovated hotel, I was encouraged to see former coworkers chatting with members of my church, gathered and ready to enjoy the festivities. A core group of my frat brothers were there as well, already at the buffet, trying to find something they liked on the vegetarian spread (*Hey, my party, no meat,* I thought!) The old school hip-hop was blasting on the over-head speaker and the room was decorated in the signature colors of black and old gold. Everyone was dressed to impress, decked out in their version of California-cool attire, and looking good.

Throwing your own party may be self-indulgent but, *You only turn fifty once,* I thought, and everyone should have the opportunity to have all your different clans of people that care about you in one room, at the same time, at an occasion besides your wedding or your funeral. I was not much of a dancer, but my brother was skilled in getting the party started. As he led my coworkers, family, church members, and frat brothers in a hyped-up version of the Electric Slide, I held my grandchildren in my arms and admired the scene in front of me. I was humbled by the kind words that were spoken and I basked in each scene, taking them in and committing them to memory. The tapestry of our lives is crafted by the sum of the relationships that have influenced us. And having those pieces of our history woven together, framed by a dance floor full of partygoers doing the Electric Slide is the definition of a good night. A very good night, indeed.

I Run Call Centers for a Living

No one grows up wanting to be a call center manager. To many, the concept of a "call center career" is an oxymoron. I was certainly no exception as my early career aspirations consisted of playing pro football or being the next Lionel Richie. Call center positions were often considered a job for slackers and I had big visions of a career filled with notoriety, travel, and wealth.

Because our mind tries to create our internal vision for ourselves, regardless of our current state, I had achieved many of these goals, some would say, in spite of my chosen career path. I had a beautiful family, money in the bank, a sweet ride, property, and upward mobility. In addition to this, I had traveled internationally and extensively, creating relationships throughout the country and literally around the world. I met some of the smartest, professional and thoughtful people due to my affiliations with call centers. In all, I had been in well over a hundred call centers, in dozens of states and six different countries either as an employee, customer, candidate, or potential buyer of call center services. By Malcom Gladwell's criteria, I was an expert in the field of contact centers several times over. I had risen from front line representative to assistant vice president in the span of twenty years acquiring what many would consider the "American Dream." All crafted one call, email, and chat at a time. Not bad for a slacker!

Although I worked a couple of call center jobs in college, I really earned my bones as a call center professional at Synergy Corporation, in Tampa. This was before the "What's in Your Pocket" campaign or "Synergy Corporation Bowl Week." During the late nineties when I joined, Syn Corp was a start-up looking to disrupt the stale credit card industry by using data such as risk profiles to customize rate offers while minimizing risk to the issuing bank. This "information-based strategy" would help Syn Corp become one of the fastest-growing companies in American business history. As a history major, my business leadership experience was limited. Synergy Corporation, however, was looking for leadership skills and more importantly, they were willing to develop your skills. I had a college degree, a finance background from retail banking and good credit. Those assets got me in the door! As I pulled up in the parking lot in a purple Ford Escort rental car provided by the company, I was laying the foundation for a successful contact center career. If you ever had the opportunity to work for a company in hyper growth mode you know that the ride can often be the best times of your career. My time at Synergy Corporation was no exception. Initially I was hired as a front line manager, leading a team of twenty phone associates who answered inbound service calls and cross sold products as an up-sell at the end of the call. I did a pretty good job in this role, but more important than my results, upper management liked the way that I achieved my results.

I was not big on business acumen or strategy but I was a motivational and inspiring leader, eager to learn and full of energy. These characteristics resonated with my team and helped me to get promoted to senior manager in a two-and-a-half-year period. The beauty of a growing organization is that the demands of growth allow people to rise to their level of incompetence. As a senior manager, I was now leading five teams, a management staff, and over a hundred representatives. Management kept investing in my skills and I kept responding, obtaining certifications from industry training programs, and attending executive training at the University of Virginia and eventually earning a Master's Degree of Arts in Organizational Management. After the company purchased a subprime auto lender in Plano, Texas, I was recruited to help that team expand their collections organization to Tampa, Florida. I was upwardly mobile and my salary reflected that; more than doubling in a few short years. *Growth is good,* I thought, never realizing that this type of growth is rare and difficult to re-capture during your career, no matter how hard you search.

During my time at Syn Corp, I purchased a painting titled *Between Gigs*. This picture depicted a group of jazz musicians jamming on their instruments as they moved through an alley from club to club. Using the painting style made famous by portraits on the seventies hit sitcom, *Good Times*, this painting still hangs in my home today. *Between Gigs* would become a metaphor for my career as I happily moved from company to company gathering diverse industry experience, corporate moves, and more money at an impressive rate. A buddy of mine, Keith Jones, recruited me to join him in Oklahoma City at a company that provided telephony solutions for businesses. I have a bit of wanderlust in me, and I could not resist the call to go west like many of my mentors.

To date, my seven and a half years at Synergy Corporation was my longest stint at any one company. On my last day in office, our site leader, Ed Siska had me sit in a conference room. He invited all the employees to stop by, shake my hand and give me kind parting words. They also created a memory book that expressed the impact I had on their careers and lives. Ed joked, that I was moving west to fulfill my lifelong desire to be a cowboy. He was part right, not about the cowboy part, but I felt my life-shaping destiny was out west. I remember driving by the complex several times before I left Tampa for Oklahoma City, actually crying as if I had lost a loved one. I actually sobbed. The leadership skills I developed as well as the relationships I created would become the foundation for each subsequent career move. Never would I feel so deeply connected to a job or a group of people. And never again would I cry when leaving a job.

My time at the Oklahoma City-based telephony company would be short-lived. I loved the idea of working for a technology company but the union environment did not fit in well with my eclectic, innovative management style. It was an important step, however, in my career growth as I got the opportunity to work with and observe my former peer, Keith Jones. Keith was an African American vice president in his mid-forties. Intelligent, reflective, and studious, this native New Yorker crystalized the model of leadership that appealed to me both from a style and a substance perspective. Keith and I were different in many ways, however, the fact that we shared cultural similarities gave me a live, walking, talking image of how I would present myself if I were a vice president of a corporation. True, I had other excellent business role models in the past.

Carey Box taught me the importance of strategic vision, Mark Suto taught me the importance of connecting with people during every interaction, Lynne Quido demonstrated the importance of deeply caring for people, and Ed Siska showed me how to "dig in" and maintain focus. But as influential as these mentors were, none of them looked like me which made it difficult for me to see myself someday taking their place. Imagery is powerful and seeing someone who looks like you in a role that you admire is a powerful motivator. Keith was that for me, and though my time working under him was short lived, it transformed the vision I had for myself and my career. After a year and a half, I was recruited to lead the largest brick-and-mortar contact center for the world's largest florist organization. I was now going to be the lead guy, not a second banana, with up to five hundred representatives and twenty mangers reporting to me. When I told Keith I was leaving, he laughed, gave a shy smile, and said, "I am proud of you man, go knock 'em dead!"

In that moment he taught me one more lesson: businesses are made to replace people. If they leave; always wish them well, and stay classy.

I Am Now In Charge

I would have gone to the ends of the earth to run my own call center, and my new job was exactly in that vicinity—near the end of the earth. 1-866Tulips.net owned a call center facility in Alamogordo, New Mexico, a town of about thirty-two thousand people. The most convenient way to get to Alamogordo is to fly into El Paso, rent a car, and drive ninety miles south, right past the Juárez, Mexico, border exit. Alamogordo is what is known as a "tertiary market." Low wages, a skilled workforce, and a modest cost of living made it an ideal place to have a contact center.

As I rode up, I realized that my first contact center was not exactly a prime cooperate real estate property. We were on the outskirts of town, beside a Dollar General on one side and a women's shelter on the other. I later learned that the building had been a grocery store in the past and my office was the old meat freezer. I had never seen actual tumbleweed before but now this weed, along with cacti and brown grass, were a normal part of the landscape. The faded purple paint on the outside of the building had seen better days as its' brilliance annually lost the battle to the New Mexico sun, wind, and sand. As my wife and I drove through the winding mountain range, using our printed MapQuest directions to find the city, my first thought was, *This is a hoax as there can't possibly be a five hundred-person call center in this town.* My second thought was, *My wife grew up in Liberty City in Miami and though she loves me, she will never follow me here and live here.* I was wrong about the first statement as there was indeed a call center in Alamogordo. I was right, however, about the second statement as my wife encouraged me to take the job but informed me that we would need to be a two-house, two-geographic location family. For the next three years, I would pursue my goal of being the chief executive of a business unit and she would visit me when she could.

To efficiently lead a retail call center organization, you have to be prepared to manage a seasonal ramp. During this period of time, you had to add temporary staff to your full-time employees to meet the increased demand of customer interactions. Most business to consumer organizations had one seasonal ramp a year: Christmas. A floral organization, however, has three short, very sharp seasonal ramps: Christmas, Valentine's Day, and Mother's Day. These ramps were specifically challenging due to the fact they only lasted a few weeks at best. Each year in Alamogordo we were tasked with going from our normal staff of roughly two hundred employees to a peak of five hundred employees the day before the holiday.

Two days later, we may hire a few of these temporary employees to full-time roles but release the rest until the next ramp season. The reputation of laying off people around the holidays as well as the low local unemployment rate added complexity to this daunting task. And though my base of employees were good people, our need to hire and release a large workforce quickly could lead to many suspect hiring decisions. As I inspected the bathrooms during an afternoon walk around the center, I picked up a spoon with a powdery residue off the men's room floor and a fifth of half-drunk dark liquor off the counter. It appears that I had interrupted a shift break with bad intentions. This would be just the first of many startling scenes that shaped my time in Alamogordo. One day, as I was walking up to the center picking up the cigarette butts that lined the front of the building, I noticed the heads of several crows neatly lined up around a large trash can. Alamogordo had a strong Wiccan community and they constantly touched base with me to let me know that they were watching what I was doing. One of my mangers informed me that he was a leader in the Wiccan community and he was using what he learned from me to create vision, strategy and how to motivate a staff for his congregation. Another one of my employees told me that the dead were observing me, through the large white board, as I gave a speech, and they approved of what I was saying. October 31 was special at my site as many office workers took the opportunity to proudly display their best witch attire. My employees did not mind working Christmas and New Year but they really needed the day that began the Winter Solstice off. Wait, there's more.

The fire department visited me during my first week to conduct a surprise inspection. They threatened several citations and warned me that they would have to shut me down if we did not bring the place up to code. I once witnessed an employee eating a slab of the biggest, "Fred Flintstone" ribs out on the call center floor. These were not boneless baby back ribs, mind you. These were the pterodactyl-style bone-in ribs that always caused Fred's car to tip over at the end of each episode. As I watched her carefully lick the barbecue sauce off her sausage-sized fingers between calls, I wondered to myself, *How do you eat a big rib like that and maintain your average handle time?* Once, a group of locals actually stole our flag off our flag pole because they said that we left it up during a rainstorm. Then there was that time when I had to layoff twelve members of the staff face-to-face. We needed to reduce cost. And as this was truly a seasonal business, this would actually be the first of several reductions in force, or RIFs, I would have to perform for Tulips. After I did the deed, a big Hispanic kid asked to meet me in the parking lot so he could whip my ass.

Luckily, I used a Jedi mind trick to talk him out it. One evening, my admin Torrey hunted me down on the call center floor scared shitless because there was a "hoopty" parked in front of the facility, playing profanity-laced rap music, and eating chicken and drinking beer. I am like, "What you want me to do about it?"

"Mr. Lyons," she replied. "You black and they black, so talk tha black shit to 'em." I took a deep breath and went out to the parking lot. As I approached the car, I got a good look at the supposed thugs in the 1987 green Cressida complete with the premium gold package upgrade. Everybody was on swole.

These are the type of black people that other black people are afraid of, I thought to myself. Luckily, they respected me due to the fact that I was in charge. I had mad swagga and I weighed four hundred plus pounds. The driver waved the peace sign at me and as he drove off, he was bumping Jay-Z's "99 Problems." Luckily, him beating my behind ain't one! I didn't even have to take off my shirt! This was all a bit overwhelming for a small-town boy from a pretty, buttoned-up background. As the leader of a New York–based company in a small town, I was exposed to cultural challenges that stretched my leadership style. These were real everyday people doing their best to provide for their families with the help of the city's largest employer after the Air Force Base, Walmart, and the local hospital. This was now my town and my people and I had no doubt that I was sent there to do great things.

My buddy Chuck Ricci always said that, "A call center, is a call center, is a call center." By this he meant that all call centers are alike. And in some ways this is accurate. Most of the people who worked there had good communication skills, strong computer skills, and generally enjoyed working with people. Most call centers had similar floor layouts as well with cubicles grouped in teams of tens, fifteens, or twenties, clustered near a team leader or supervisor. The center of attention was normally a wall of monitors displaying inbound and outbound call activity. With conference rooms on the perimeter of the floor, the sterile, professional decor was often disrupted with bright and colorful pictures, stickers, stars, and certificates. Because call center work is often repetitive, management attempted to distract workers from the monotony by decorating the office to resemble a nursery or a kindergarten class room. Sure there were posters with goals, vision, and performance scorecards but the best contact centers looked like a hodgepodge of old Christmas lights and a community art class. Up to this point in my career, I had worked in call centers in Alexandria, Virginia; Tampa, Florida; Plano, Texas; and Oklahoma City, and to Chuck's point, there were many similarities.

The largest employee in a tertiary market, like 1-866-Tulips. net, however, brought on unique challenges. Being the leader of one of the small town's largest employers also meant that I was on constant display as well. I actually walked up on a group of people talking about me, actually saying my name repeatedly before they realized that I was right behind them. It was like being famous without the money! Since my call center was open twenty-four hours a day, I decided to make a surprise visit to the center at midnight to ensure people were productive. I went to the back of the building and walked up on what could only be described as circus-like atmosphere. The lights were dim, incense was burning, and someone was holding a puppy! I had to runoff all the nonemployees who were just hanging out and fixed the flood lights to restore a normal working environment.

Call centers are filled with real people and they bring their real issues to work. Every once in a while, a sheriff would come to my door asking to meet one of my employees so they could serve them papers involving a legal matter. On one occasion, I was called to the front of the site to retrieve an employee and I refused based on call volume. I informed him that he could come back at the associate's lunchtime or during the employee's afternoon break. Ten minutes later, the sheriff came back and served me a warrant for obstructing justice. I think he was just trying to scare me as I was never actually arrested for the matter. Some memories are etched in my mind as once in a lifetime experiences. The site was neat and clean but the lobby furniture was pretty dilapidated. I received word that a small contact center in the city was closing shop. Our vice president said that we could buy the furniture as long as I could get it to the site. This excited my management team so they all showed up with their trucks in front of the building and we personally moved three rooms of lobby furniture into the building. I thought to myself, this type of thing can only happen when you are outside of the Fortune 500!

Two and a half years in, we were making great strides as a team. After creating a vision, mission, values, and some key staff removals and replacements, we became a competitive call center leadership team. Managing a stand-alone call center thousands of mile away from corporate was like being the mayor of a small town. Although our cultures and backgrounds were different, I was truly enjoying the people and it reflected in the way that we treated each other. My family and I were seeing each other only once every three months or so, so this left time for me to participate on local boards, mentor kids, and play a role in the local chamber of commerce events. I even spoke on behalf of the company at two funerals during my time in Alamogordo. I was far from home and missed my family but we were creating a legacy that, I believed, would last longer than my time there. Just when I got comfortable with the responsibilities of the center and juggling my personal accountabilities, the business did what businesses do—changed!

A new management team in New York took over the direction of the contact center organization. Though we were striving locally, our brick-and-mortar model in small tertiary markets were draining local talent and making it difficult to fill our labor needs to meet our three seasonal ramps, year after year. Instead of adjusting our labor rate, we decided to outsource 60 percent of our labor force to countries with low costs and large populations of educated English speakers. We would eventually close all but one of our brick-and-mortar contact centers allowing the majority of our representatives the opportunity to work from home. This was great for these employees as they were on the cutting edge of telecommuting and setting the groundbreaking path for the future of work. It was a complete restructuring of the organization and I was fortunate to be asked to lead the new business processing outsourcer or BPO, vendor model. I feared that I was going to be fired as a result of the shake-up but I was actually promoted! My new title was "Director of Global Customer Care" and in this new role I would have Account Managers accountable for the performance of our vendor relationships. This team would grow from a couple of hundred workers in off peak to well over a thousand during ramp seasons. The Outsource Companies were based in Central and South America as well as Asia. In thirteen short years, I had gone from managing twenty phone representatives locally to selecting, contracting, onboarding, and managing the performance of seven vendor partners in five countries and ten cities. Although this outsourcing was vilified in certain business circles, it was readily adopted by most large organizations as a viable business strategy. My new boss, Mark Phurman, looked at me and said, "Have you ever traveled out of the US?"

I said, "Sure, I have been to Jamaica!" He responded with a slight laugh.

Mark, a world traveler, then said, "I am going to take you to Central America with me and show you the ropes and then you need to go to the Philippines on your own."

"Sure, Mark, no problem and thanks for the opportunity." I remember looking at the map for Guatemala and thinking, *Okay, this is like going to South Texas.* Then I looked for the Philippines, and I swallowed hard, initially intimidated by the distance. I got over that quickly. I had never used the term "dream job" before, but this was it. I used to say that I dreamed of not needing a job, but traveling, building new relationships, and leading people were all things that I loved.

Mark suggested that I get a copy of the book *The World is Flat: A Brief History of the Twenty-First Century* by *New York Times* columnist Thomas Friedman. This was prior to owning a Kindle or an iPad, so I lugged this 1,100-page book on the plane for my first twenty-one-hour trip to the Philippines. In this book, the writer expertly explains why it was more cost-effective to send calls to Manila than small-town USA:

> What happened over the last years is that there was a massive investment in technology, especially in the bubble era, when hundreds of millions of dollars were invested in putting broadband connectivity around the world, undersea cables, all those things." At the same time, he added, computers became cheaper and dispersed all over the world, and there was an explosion of e-mail software, search engines like Google and proprietary software that can chop up any piece of work and send one part to Boston, one part to Bangalore and one part to Beijing, making it easy for anyone to do remote development.

I was catching the end of a trend of outsourcing contact center jobs requiring English skills. Of course, we were not the only company doing this as large corporations were exploring lower-cost,

English-speaking workers all across the globe. This worked specifically well for our industry as it required a large force of temporary workers several times a year, for very short bursts of time. Americans had more of an appetite for full-time work and the students overseas enjoyed the short stints of employment around their studies. In addition to this, call center work was more valued in these international communities, paying a livable wage, as well as affording young adults career advancement opportunities. Technology, low labor costs, and large tranches of English speakers flattened the corporate landscape and led to globalization.

My first trip overseas was with Mark to Central America. For one week, we would fly into Guatemala, take an in-country flight from Guatemala to El Salvador and end our trip with a short stay in Costa Rica. We traveled with Roberto who was the head of IT. Mark and I made quite an interesting pair, traveling through the airport representing opposite ends of the spectrum both physically and stylistically. During this time, I was tipping the scale at nearly four hundred pounds. I tended to move, let's just say, *deliberately* and I spoke that way as well. Mark was five-foot-five and 120 pounds, soaking wet. He was a fast-talker, shooting from the hip, and pretty unstructured. Mark traveled extensively in prior roles and he loved showing the ropes to international travel virgins like me.

When we arrived at the Marriott in San José, Costa Rica, Mark was greeted by the doorman with a warm "Welcome back, Mr. Phurman." and a hearty smile. A bellman then rolled a small four-wheeled bag out to Mark. "Your luggage, Mr. Phurman."

"Thanks, sir," Mark replied. I am not sure exactly what was in that black bag or why they kept it in the back, but it established Mark's presence with me in Central America and that he was quite a character, someone to look up to and Costa Rica was his playground.

After a week of hosting performance reviews, meeting the teams at each center, and intercountry travel, I was ready to turn in early and prepare for my flight back home. Mark, however, had other ideas.

"Darren, we are going to a casino in downtown Costa Rica to finish off your first trip."

"Hey, Mark," I said, "I appreciate the gesture but I would be a boring companion as I don't really drink, smoke, or gamble."

"Wow," Mark replied, "You promote a black guy and he won't even drink with you." We had a quick laugh but then Mark insisted that I tag along anyway just to be part of the team. Mark could be very persuasive! Escorted by our in-country partner Dirk, and a bodyguard, Mark. Roberto and I pulled up to a small casino attached to a large hotel in downtown San José. Dirk was quite the character as well. Simultaneously, he cussed like a rapper and quoted scripture like a preacher. In his mid-forties, he had staked his claim in this beautiful country of Costa Rica, enjoying the fruits of his labor. Tall, charismatic, and lean, one of his claims to fame was dating the much younger Miss Costa Rica. Mark and Dirk headed directly to the blackjack tables and left Roberto and I to fend for ourselves. As we walked around the room, I noticed that there were lots of women in the lobby, tons of women. Like five for every man present. They were all very attractive as well, dressed scantily, and smiling while saying hi to us.

I thought to myself, "*Wow, heavyset black guys must be a rarity here in Costa Rica because I am getting a lot of attention.*" As we smiled and nodded our way to the bar, a woman came up to us and rubbed her hand gently against my shoulder. This caress seemed a bit unusual and at that moment I came out of my trance and realized that the casino, attached to the hotel, was actually a full-service brothel! That's why there were dozens of attractive woman for every man! That's why they were all pretty, and that's why they were all smiling at me. It was not because I looked like a fat Denzel Washington, it was because I looked like a fat paycheck. At that moment, I went out to the alley and called my wife.

"Honey," I said. "I just want to let you know that I am in a brothel, love you, and see you tomorrow."

My thought process was that I would certainly share this story with everyone and I did not want my wife hearing about this during casual conversation. As I went back into the "casino" and grabbed my ginger ale from the bar, I caught a glimpse of Mark, Dirk and Roberto all laughing at my reaction to my discovery. The experience was sort of an initiation and it confirmed me as the world's most boring international travel partner.

A week later, I boarded Philippine Air at LAX for my first flight to Asia. As I stuffed my four-hundred-plus pound body into my coach seat. I considered the route that I would take to get to Manila. Oklahoma City to Los Angeles, Los Angeles to Toronto, and Toronto to Manila. In subsequent trips, I would travel from Oklahoma City to Houston, Houston to Honolulu, Honolulu to Guam, and Guam to Manila. Oklahoma City to Minneapolis, Minneapolis to Japan, and Japan to Manila was popular as well. I was pretty sure that no one was ever intended to travel from Oklahoma City to Manila. During over a dozen or so trips to our partners on the islands, I tried each of these routes as they were all about twenty hours of total flight time. Up through this period of my life, I had not flown more than three to four hours in one flight. As I finished off the 1100th page of *The World is Flat*, I reflected on how my life had profoundly changed in the past few years. I had been an average student at best with a night school master's degree from a for-profit institution.

Not the stuff that great careers are made of, I thought. I grew up in a small southern town to a factory worker and a hospital secretary. They used their modest resources to give my brother and I a stable upbringing giving us the best advantages that they could afford. A safe home and a college education launched us to solid careers and gave us the foundation to build families of our own. Now, I was adding distinction to this by becoming a world traveler. Darren Lyons, international businessman!

"That has a great ring to it," I thought. As I waited for the shuttle to take me to my hotel, I breathed in the warm night air of the Manila International Airport. Despite the cost, I called my father and said, "Dad, I wanted to let you know that I landed. Your baby boy is on the other side of the world!"

The desire for upward mobility, newer stuff, and more money can corrupt your sense of accomplishment and lead you to make career choices that do not line up with your true values. Financially well-off people always advise you to never make career decisions based on money. "Do something you love and you will never work a day in your life," and "Money can't buy you happiness." All this is solid advice, however, it is wasted on the ears of the less affluent. When you grow up modestly and begin to build your career, you have a number and a title in mind and that number and title, unfortunately, can lead you to step away from your dream job to pursue more for just the purpose of having more. More can also mask the things that truly bring you happiness as well. "More" is an alluring mistress. That's what happened to me. I loved what I was doing. I had built a team of ten people all across the country that managed my partners all across the world. I had about thirty people that I sent to my partners three times a year to support our seasonal ramps. I personally traveled monthly to our headquarters in Long Island to discuss strategy with our top leadership. I also traveled to each of our partners in Guatemala, El Salvador, Costa Rica, Guyana, and the Philippines several times a year to strengthen performance and relationships. Because the company had an entrepreneurial spirit, I was given full autonomy over my organization. I enjoyed the complete confidence of top leadership as I was never micro-managed or even questioned about my budget or my actions in general. The only problem is that I did not have the "number" or my "title" that was in my mind and those factors made me open to distractions. I was constantly being recruited through LinkedIn by organizations looking for strong leaders with contact center skills. When a world-class property and casualty, Fortune 200 company reached out offering a promotion and significantly more money. I could not resist. Much like those musicians in my *Between Gigs* painting, I was going to take my instruments to a new gig, with the title of assistant vice president and $25,000 additional dollars. I went from being "The Tulip Boy" to an African American executive for one of the oldest, most prestigious companies in America. Furthermore, their local offices were literally five miles from home in Oklahoma City.

This was my destiny, I thought, not realizing that I was being led by my ambitions and not my values. I already had the dream scenario as 1-866-Tulips.net that was perfect for me. I just got distracted.

Large Fortune 200 companies have the best of everything. The best people, the best facilities, the best technology, and the funding.

The Spirit of the Stagg Insurance was no exception as the tools, people, and resources I was exposed to during that time matched the similar capabilities I had experienced during my time at Syn Corp. Rich in tradition, my corner office was decked out in sturdy wood furniture with framed replica reproductions of both Robert E. Lee and Abraham Lincoln's insurance policies hanging on the walls.

"That was a far cry from the converted meat locker office I had during their time in Alamogordo." I thought to myself. The people were awesome as well as in my new role I had executive responsibility for the local site in Oklahoma City as well as accountability for five hundred licensed insurance agents across four US sites.

Just a natural progression of position, money, and responsibility, I thought to myself as I tried to not become overwhelmed by the weight of the role. If the opportunity in Alamogordo was akin to being mayor of a small town, then my new role was like being a city councilman in a large metropolis. Large companies, however, had cultural aspects that I did not anticipate when I left my dream position at Tulips. A large, layered vertical corporate structure, a rigid change management process, and a tradition of resistance to transformational change challenged the characteristics of autonomy and creativity that I enjoyed so much in prior roles. My manager once told me that, "Autonomy is an allusive pursuit, my friend." Never have truer words been spoken.

The Stagg had tons of talented people and each one of them had insights, experience and opinions that needed to be considered prior to implementing any change. In prior roles it had been me and a few well-meaning team members against the world. The entrepreneurial spirit at 1-866-Tulips.net demanded that you get your hands dirty as you were constantly challenged with delivering excellent results with thin budgets and few resources. I thrived in this environment. At the Stagg, there was an abundance of people and money and they required that you use company protocol to initiate any significant initiative. This was often in contradiction to my creative, shoot from the hip style that had served me well in smaller or growing organizations. The environment was also dedicated to a strict performance management philosophy that required that you "stack rank" your management team on a performance curve and often times "manage out" the lowest performers. This Jack Welch–based philosophy created a lion-and-gazelle culture where, in order to survive, you had to be faster than slowest gazelle or the slowest lion in order to survive.

Even good people can be transformed into predators if you reward the right behaviors. The people who thrived in this type organization were often indigenous to that environment, they knew where the bodies were buried and were skilled in the art of survival. As I was challenged to "manage up or out" many of the top leadership on my team, my job satisfaction decreased with each termination. During my three years there, the structure of senior leadership team changed at least three times. This brought on a change in strategy, a change in direction, and constant changes in talent. As I watched the people I liked the most leave the organization, I lost myself again and slipped into a depression, needing to talk myself out of bed each morning to make it through the day. "Money and title" had captured another victim; briefly stripping me of my confidence and robbing me of my joy. For the first time in a decade I had no idea where I was going in my career, no goals and no real sense of purpose.

My time at the Stagg was defined by extreme career highs and extreme career lows. During a week-long trip to our main offices in Connecticut, my boss requested that I cut my trip short to meet with members of our Senior Leadership team back in Oklahoma City. Moore, Oklahoma had recently experienced a Category 5 Tornado that had severely impacted the lives and property of Stagg employees and customers. Members of the senior leadership team wanted to tour the area and show support to the local employees in the field. I thought this was a wonderful gesture so I quickly agreed to cutting my trip short. The only problem was actually finding a flight home on such short notice.

"Darren, you can just fly on the corporate jet with us," my boss said. Outwardly, I very calmly, and coolly accepted the offer. Inwardly, I was dancing a strange combination of the cabbage patch and the running man!

"I didn't even know we had a corporate jet!" I thought. I could not believe that I was actually going to be flying private. I remember

the first time that I flew business class and thinking, *I am never going to go back to flying coach again.* This, however, was on another level. As the car service took me to the private regional airport, I made my way to the small lounge.

Once there, I was greeted by the pilot, "Hello, my name is Roger and I am your pilot, here is my identification. Can I see your identification please?" After this ritual, I was escorted to the plane with my seven or so travel companions. They were all accustomed to this mode of travel but I was doing my best not to appear as impressed with the surroundings as I actually was. As I settled in my seat, I was startled by how quickly the pre-takeoff procedure took when you fly privately. I quickly removed my personal seat belt extension from my bag and buckled up. Tipping the scale at 350, a personal seatbelt was a handy accessory to have around. Over the past five years, I had flown well over a hundred thousand miles both domestically and internationally but private flight was special. Normally, you cannot wait for a flight to be over. This one, however, ended way too quickly.

I can honestly say that I experienced the lowest point of my career at the Stagg as well. I had been with the company a little over a year. During that time, I had worked an average of sixty hours a week, which consisted primarily of hours and hours of back-to-back conference calls. I had traveled extensively between our four sites, spending time in hotels and away from my family. I had a couple of successes in redesigning some performance criteria that drove sales but primarily I suffered many setbacks in trying to adjust my style to the corporate culture. I consistently met and tripped over obstacles in the culture, losing confidence, and cache along the way. I remember once going into the office on a Sunday and working for eight hours to prepare a four-page deck for my boss. Routinely, I held two-hour meetings with multiple members of my team just to prepare for a fifteen-minute presentation during our monthly business reviews. I was all in as the financial rewards and benefits were like nothing I had ever imagined. I thought it was all worth it when my boss gave me my review and shared my new compensation package for the coming year.

"Darren, she said, your new salary is $164, 000, and because of company performance, you will receive a $50,000 cash bonus. All told, your salary, bonus, and long-term stock incentives, are equivalent to just under a quarter million dollars in total compensation. Your bonus and salary increase will be on your next check."

I quickly thanked her and left the room, before she changed her mind. I would have to stay several more years to receive the long-term stock incentives but the fifty thousand bonus would be in my account in less than fourteen days. Fifty thousand was equivalent to a signing bonus for minor league professional athlete I thought. All the work, the tough conversations, the long nights, the trying my best to fit into the corporate culture was worth it. What should have been the best day of my career turned into the worst day. Nothing can kill the exuberance of a cash bonus like taxes. With federal and state taxes deducted a $50,000 quickly turns into a $30,000 bonus. Thirty thousand dollars is nothing to sneeze at but it is certainly a lot less than what you expect. Taxes are a gut punch and it makes you think about all those things that your affluent friends said, "Never take a job for the money," "Money can't buy you happiness," etc. Now I truly understood what they were talking about. When you work for money and not for satisfaction, the money is the only thing that you are guaranteed to get. You have to ask yourself, "Is the squeeze worth the juice?"

For six months or so, my depressed state reflected in my work. I showed up every day but my heart was not in it. As I struggled to fit in, the conversations with my boss became tougher and tougher. When I came to the company, my hiring was celebrated by my colleagues as there were few African Americans at the VP level, especially in operations. Now, I was hesitant, unsure of myself and it showed in my performance. We were miles away from the heights of riding the corporate jet. I became "the slowest gazelle," in danger of being devoured by the pride of lions. The company's commitment to a strict rack-and-stack culture placed a target on my back. I was now the slowest lion, destined to die of starvation because I could not capture the slowest gazelle. During my midyear review, my boss informed me that if my performance did not improve, I would be rated below satisfactory and not be eligible for a salary increase, bonus, or incentives. This less-than-satisfactory rating would certainly leave me vulnerable to being released if management positions needed to be reduced due to budgetary cut backs.

"I would be first on the list," I thought. This environment had chewed up and spit out other talented people and I felt like I was headed for same fate. I thought to myself, *"How could I have fallen off so quickly?"* Coupled with this, I was struggling hiding the stress from my team. Several of my employees observed that I rarely laughed and smiled any more. I was also losing weight at a rapid pace. When I met my wife, I weighed 465 pounds. Through a low carb diet, I had gotten down to 390 pounds. The Monday after Thanksgiving 2010, after eating an embarrassing amount of turkey, I decided to forgo meat for a while. My system must have liked this as I immediately began to lose weight.

Four short years later, my new weight hovered at around three hundred pounds. Before my illness, I would get down to just under 265 pounds. That's over two-hundred-pound total loss! Warren Sapp once referred to his sixty-pound weight loss as "losing a fifth grader." Well, by Warren's standards, I had lost a full grown man! The stress, no doubt, escalated the weight loss. This new physique resulted in a new wardrobe but not a better quality of life. I spent more and more time isolated from friends and family, in my man cave watching cable television. I spent more and more time at work and less and less time with friends and family. I even stopped watching the NFL. If you had told me that I would be at my lowest weight in over twenty years and I was making much more money than I could have ever imagined and still be unhappy; I would have said that you were delusional. That was, none the less, the case. As I tried to work my way out of my funk, I was constantly reminded of my precarious situation. If the one-on-ones with my manger were not tough enough, on three separate occasions senior leaders mentioned that they were aware of the tough conversations between me and my boss. When I asked one of them if he thought I could pull out of this decline he stated, "You will either be managed up or managed out. Either way, you will be okay." This was certainly not inspiring. I was a gazelle surrounded by the pride of lions with only one option; I had to change jungles.

LinkedIn is a great tool as it allows you to broadcast your best professional qualities to the world. This professional social media tool, allows you to craft your career story, and passively make yourself available to recruiters anxious to steal you away from your current role for their clients seeking top talent. I always said that I wanted to elevate my career to a level where if I had to take a step back, the falloff in money and title would not be too dramatic. Because of LinkedIn, that opportunity came to me and I decided to leave the Stagg for a privately owned company.

At this company, I would manage domestic and international operations for the second largest retail florist in the country. Although the title was a step down and the company was not world-class like the Stagg, a familiar industry and comparable compensation appealed to me and it was a nice landing place for my next career move, whatever that was. The hiring was quite dramatic as I finished work one evening and flew from Oklahoma to Los Angeles in preparation for an interview with the CEO and the COO who would be my direct supervisor. After several connecting flights, I put my head on the pillow of a plush local hotel at midnight local time. In eight hours, I would have the next biggest interviews of my career.

"Six hours of sleep and I just need to be perfect for two or three hours," I thought to myself. The company offered to bring me in as senior director and promote me in role to vice president if the business grew. A smaller company with the opportunity for growth sounded like a perfect level of risk/reward for my career. Since the operation was less than ten miles from my house in Oklahoma City, the transition would be pretty easy so I accepted the position. As I left the Stagg, I realized that I had let an awesome opportunity slip through my fingers. I was an assistant vice president of a world-class organization, complete with all the trappings afforded to the position. Unfortunately, I could not get excited about the work and without excitement I was an average employee at best.

After a year and a half with my new company, my boss called me one day and said, "Darren, the vice president position that I hired you for is no longer available to you. I am not sure what to do with you so let's agree to think about it over the next couple of weeks and discuss further the next time I am in town."

The words hung in the air long after the call disconnected. After twenty years of successfully avoiding several reductions in force (RIFs), layoffs, restructures, closings, and reorganizations, I finally got snagged by this midlife rite of passage. The company was not growing and the industry was changing. Either way, my current employer could no longer support a senior position over this organization. They would eventually replace me with a junior-level contributor close contact center operations in Oklahoma City and centralize all operations in a tertiary market out of state. I was once again "between gigs" but for the first time, it was not by my choosing. I watched several talented colleagues get "caught" in an organizational restructuring. It happens and has sort of become a mid-life rite of passage. By observation, I noticed that the people who transitioned the best kept a positive attitude, did not take it personally and maintained their dignity throughout the process. I tried not to think about the fact that I was brought into this organization with much fanfare. I tried not to think about the fact that my boss and I had discussed me replacing her on several occasions, I tried not to think about the fact that I had left a Fortune 200 company for this opportunity, and I tried not to focus on the fact that I was less than thirty days removed from the heights of my fiftieth birthday celebration.

Don't take it personal. Do your research, know your rights, and just let it happen, I thought. After tough conversations, we agreed that I would leave within the next sixty days. This time, there was no real safety net and I would have to figure out my next move. I was confident that I could find a comparable position but I was hesitant to rush into another organization.

During my fiftieth birthday party, two of my fraternity brothers had pitched me the opportunity to join a company that they were starting. I would run operations for their new start-up as COO for Alekto. The company was pre-revenue and pre-client, which meant that there would initially be no compensation. It seemed like the perfect time for this risk, as I had a little money in the bank and I needed a break from the traditional corporate grind. Plus, I was confident in my ability to quickly find a job if Alekto did not work out. In my mind, I had been preparing for this opportunity my entire life.

Once funded, I would be on the ground floor of unlimited earning potential and the opportunity to help build an organization reflective of the best cultures I had experienced as I moved "between gigs." The opportunity to work with friends was icing on the cake. This was a logical next step and a chance to accelerate the legacy I wanted to build for my grandchildren. I never anticipated that this would be the first of several life changing rites of passage that would change my life forever.

Alekto

In July 2016, Philando Castile was shot and killed by a St. Paul, Minnesota, police officer after disclosing that he possessed a firearm. The tragedy gained national prominence due to his girlfriend live streaming the events immediately following the shooting via Facebook.

I watched as many black men in my network struggled to go to work as they grappled with feelings of anger and fear; contemplating how to interact with police officers during routine traffic stops when they follow all the rules. By all accounts, Philando was a good brother just trying to get home after a hard day's work. It was against this background that Walter, James, and I embarked on the journey of building a new, innovative internet service company that would disrupt the credit reporting industry. Walter, an MBA and self-described cool geek, had been working on bringing this service to market for the past decade or so. Walter had sunk all his worldly possessions into this effort; sleeping on sofas between family and his girlfriend's apartment. He was the founder, CEO, and tech head of the group. James, who I had known since I was eighteen, was the chief revenue officer. After a decade as vice president of sales for a large BPO organization, James was sinking his efforts and his severance into selling this new company to potential clients and investors. Much like me, James was taking a break from traditional corporate America, attempting to transition to an entrepreneurial mind-set.

Tall, charming, and handsome, James had the innate ability to find common ground with anyone. I always marveled at his ability to have meaningful conversation about any subject. As COO, I would bring all my process knowledge to the Alekto's go-to market strategy.

Eventually, I would build and manage an operation that would service our customers. Once we had customers. We were an impressive leadership team. Walter was the experienced start-up vet who had participated in several organizations transitioning from embryonic idea to fully funded corporation. Tired of always being a "bridesmaid and never a bride" in the financial technology start-up, get rich quick era, Walter, a perfectionist by nature, was determined to make this iteration of the Alekto executive team work in making his tech start-up dreams come true. We were a talented team, and I was convinced that there was big money willing to invest in our abilities and experience. As we went about our daily scrum meetings, building our processes, and strategies, Walter, James, and I felt fortunate to have each other as we struggled with the dichotomy and feelings of angst that saw three black executives join forces to build a thriving business in a country that still saw black men as a threat to society even when they followed the laws of the land. It is very difficult to feel both simultaneously empowered and insignificant, emboldened yet afraid. That, however, was the environment as we prepared for our first meeting with a potential investor.

Walter and James had been attempting to set up a meeting with a fraternity brother of ours, Maverick Bryant, who we knew from college days. Maverick had worked for Microsoft in the nineties, helping the fledgling company bring several of their key strategies to market. He had built a fortune through technology and now held a position of managing partner working for Winston Ellison at Valliant Investment Partners. My first move as Alekto's COO was landing a face-to-face with Maverick on the thirty-first floor of his offices in downtown Austin, Texas. The large conference room windows opened up to the Texas State Capital Building. The impressive, high-tech setting was professionally accented with both sleek designs and Texan embellishments. This was truly a "mountaintop moment" much like my trip in the corporate jet. As Walter, James, and I anxiously awaited Maverick's arrival, my eyes darted between the view outside and the oversized painting of a Stetson dominating the northern conference room wall. The room was obviously designed to intimidate the visitor and, I must admit, the surroundings were accomplishing the intent of their creation. Maverick entered the room and immediately put us at ease. Walter, James, and Maverick had been close in school sharing many fond memories together. He and I had been cordial, as I knew him as a young man wanting to pledge my fraternity.

Now the three of us were coming to him, hat in hand, openly riding the shield in search of his advice, guidance, influence, but most importantly, his money.

James and I were definitely on a timer, counting down the days and the money until we would have to go back on the traditional job market. We both watched on as Walter presented the business strategy of Alekto to Maverick, presenting our case as to why he should sink some of his hard-earned money into our nontraditional offering. Expertly and politely, Maverick gently poked holes in our business case. With the professional dexterity of someone who reviewed business plans for a living and the kindness of a sympathetic friend, Maverick listened for twenty minutes or so before suggesting that we join him for a "drinky-drink" back at his residence in the hills of Austin. As we pulled up to his palatial estate, my four-year-old BMW would be the runt of his impressive exotic car collection. Walter, James, and I desperately tried to keep our cool all day and not be too blown away by Maverick's success. Even Walter got giddy, however, as he asked Maverick if he could take a selfie in his late model McLaren. As I reflect back on that day, I am reminded of my journal entry that night back at the hotel:

> I can't unsee the awesome display of success and wealth that I experienced during my time with Maverick Bryant in Austin.
>
> It is not as much about meeting him on the thirty-first floor of the Frost Building overlooking the Capitol in downtown Austin, or visiting his eleven-thousand-square-foot home or the four or six cars, it is the four-to-five staff members that he employs to care for his estate and family; four-to-five by my count. It is about his ability to personally sponsor an AAU team for his son so that he can play against the best competition.

It is about his ability to send his kids to the best schools based on his specifications.

It is about his ability to give a substantial donation to that school to help shape the environment, and ultimately, the future of other children.

It is about his ability to give a neighbor a million-dollar investment to help their dreams come true.

It is about MB having the resources to carve out the life he desires for him and his family.

My paradigm has shifted.

My ideas of success have been challenged and detonated.

My possibilities have been reassessed; they are now endless.

God, enlarge my territory.

The best way to explain it is looking at your local lake and it being your picture of beauty. It is scenic and awe-inspiring. Then you visit the Grand Canyon and though your local lake is still beautiful, the boundaries of beauty, its majesties and brilliance have been challenged, enlarged, broadened. *You can't unsee it!* And the local lake is beautiful, but it can no longer be your standard of beauty.

Maverick did not fund Alekto. He was encouraging but said that he could not get excited about the business model. He politely asked for more information but ultimately, he declined our offer to get involved with our business. This should have been a sign that our idea needed a great deal more development and that it was not quite ready for consumption. Much like other entrepreneurs, however, this setback inspired us to double down on our efforts. And though we did not achieve our initial intent, the time with Maverick left us on an emotional high and more confident in our purpose and our vision even if the path forward was not clear. As we prepared for our first executive off-site at a ski resort in Virginia, the dream team intended to build on this experience and further develop our strategy.

Elaine and I packed up my Beemer and began the twenty-one-hour drive from Oklahoma City to Massanutten, Virginia. We donated our time-share to host the first of what I hoped would be an annual Alekto executive off-site strategy planning session. James was based in Richmond, Virginia, and Walter was spending the majority of his time in the North Carolina Research Triangle. With the exception of a couple of weekends and our visit with Maverick, the off-site would represent our first extended exposure to each other as we continued to refine our business and subsequently find clients and funding. I was looking forward to our time on the east coast, and Elaine and I intended to visit some family on the front and back end of our business meetings. Admittedly, Alekto had lost some momentum after our unsuccessful meeting with Maverick but this off-site, I thought, would give us the shot in the arm to forge ahead with our grand plans. As the organizer of the meetings, my thought was after three or four days together, Walter, James, and I would surely leave this "genius time" with a game plan to move forward. I know that James and I were growing concerned with our ability to resist the call to get a job. Although we were not panicking, our funds continued to dwindle. Our women were supportive but at some point they would tire of being the primary breadwinners. We discussed this from time to time as we poured our best efforts into the business. The off-site, we thought, would help set us on the right path and help us pivot our business plan. For four days, Walter, James, and I met and redefined the Alekto business plan and valuation. Maverick had asked for specific information and, at the time, we still held out hope that he would take an active role in our business. With the Shenandoah Valley as a picturesque backdrop, the three of us hammered away on our matching MacBooks working at the condo dining room table at night and Starbucks by day. So cliché. Our different styles and business perspectives often led to thoughtful conversation and debate which often ended in good natured ribbing and reflective reminiscing of college days. Walter, a true techy and perfectionist at heart, often butted heads with James and my more fluid management styles. We worked, we laughed, we joked but mostly we dreamed about the day we would be funded, hire staff and open our first brick-and-mortar offices. I was not getting paid and growing anxious about my shrinking savings but, admittedly, I was having the time of my life. Everyone should have the opportunity to work with friends. Successful or not, it can be a liberating and learning experience, and create memories that can inspire you for the rest of your career.

If you ever have been around an unfunded start-up near the holidays, then you are familiar with this particular cross section of fear, desperation, and isolation. All activity slowed to a distinct crawl, call backs ceased, and isolation mounted as people got more busy with the holidays and less concerned with your start-up dreams. Meetings with established businesses to discuss how your service can benefit their organization began to cancel; slipping down the priority list as leaders become distracted with parties and other festive activities. As a struggling entrepreneur, you feel like the guy on the outside looking into the snow globe. It looks like fun inside the globe but you are stuck on the outside. The conversations I began to have with some recruiters came to a grinding halt as the season did not bode well for interview schedules. Based in different states, Walter, James, and I didn't even have each other to share our misery and disappointment.

Our daily SPRINT meetings became less focused and attendance reflecting all three of us at the same time was spotty. As each of us juggled our personal disappointment and regret, our interactions became less frequent; well-mannered, but short. If the meeting with Maverick and the off-site at Massanutten were the Alekto high, the holidays were a new low. I tried to put on a brave face for Elaine but I had to break the news to her that we would need to dip into my 401(k) at the end of the year. She was supportive as I explained that we had given Alekto seven months but we were no closer to getting a client or funding than when we started. As the new year began, I realized that I would have to put a pause on my entrepreneurial dreams and reenter the job market. We had given it a good try, and I had learned a lot of lessons that I would take with me back into corporate America. Once again, between gigs.

The Incident

In Oklahoma, there is an old saying, "if you don't like the weather, then give it a minute and it will change." The winter of 2017 brought in career opportunities and possibilities along with an early January ice storm. Oklahoma is infamous for ice storms and a couple of inches of this menace can paralyze the metro area for days. While putting on snow boots, I cut the heel of my left foot. Not thinking much of it, I continued to slip on my favorite boots and ventured out into the winter weather to meet my wife for lunch.

I was in the middle of the job hunt of my life, reviewing my resume, and sending it out to several recruiters. I was trying to maximize my time with my wife before heading back into the job market. During my downtime, I was also walking at one of the neighborhood malls, trying to maintain my weight loss and increase my strength. Later that night, I removed my snow boot and noticed the cut on my foot looked worse and the skin of my heel was beginning to separate from my foot. I briefly thought about going to the doctor or the emergency room, but immediately dismissed the thought.

"No time for that," I thought. I went up to my man cave bathroom, got some alcohol and a Band-Aid, and self-administered first aid to my injured left foot. Briefly, I considered the fact that I was a diabetic and injuries to my feet could have grave consequences. But stubbornly, I dismissed reason and decided to wait until morning to take further action. I also decided to keep this injury a secret from my wife.

"No need to bother her with this," I thought to myself. The next day, I checked my foot and thought it was no worse for wear so

I rewrapped it and put on my red University of Phoenix athletic socks and went for a two-mile walk in the mall. The walk was slow and deliberate but I persevered through the pain. I stopped by the store and purchased more Band-Aids and alcohol to continue my self-medication. Day after day I repeated this ritual, retreating to my man cave, checking my foot, assessing the damage, and administering my version of first aid. Each day I was making my assessment, does the foot look better or worse? Was the pain worse today when I removed my sock? Is that smell new or more rank than yesterday? Is the source of the odor the foot, or just the fact that I have been walking two miles a day without taking a shower because I did not want to get my foot wet?

Although I tried my best to avoid her, my wife commented on my smell as this ritual went on for four weeks. I should have gone to the doctor weeks ago, but now I convinced myself that I was in too deep. One day after a two mile walk, I felt and heard a distinct *crack* in my left heel. It felt as if my entire ankle disintegrated as I limped into the house. Foolishly, I convinced myself that I had badly twisted my ankle. I, once again, retreated to my man cave to sleep it off, convinced that it would be better in the morning. It was not until the next day, barely able to walk, that I decided to go to urgent care. Reluctantly, I removed my left sneaker to let the aide examine my foot.

"Did you drive here by yourself?" she asked inquisitively.

"Yes," I said defiantly. She immediately helped me put my left shoe back on and strongly suggested that I drive myself to emergency room to have my foot examined by a specialist. As I limped back to the car I thought to myself, *"How bad can this be if she did not put me in an ambulance to go to the emergency room but allowed me to drive myself there?"*

Still in denial. Reflecting back, I have learned to never trust the stories that you tell yourself in the midst of your own health crisis. The initial onslaught of an injury or diagnosis of a condition can chip away at the logic of your self-talk, reducing you to your best high hopes or your worst fear regarding your condition. An outside assessment would give you critical information to consider and balance your internal dialogue. In other words, don't be so afraid of the worst consequences that you neglect to consider additional rational opinions. The ability to pause your fears and rationally consider additional data can successfully navigate any life challenge. Unfortunately, I lacked this ability during the most critical moments of my health crisis. My self-talk did me in.

The bright lights of an emergency room examination pod can leave you dazed and confused. As I opened my eyes, I made out three distinct figures; one was my wife and the other two I came to know as an orthopedic surgeon, Dr. Davenport, and the on call Podiatrist, Dr. Harper. Although the three of them were meeting for the first time, they shared the same facial expression; furrowed brow and hand to chin, contemplating how to tell a fifty-year-old man that his life was going to change forever. The foot that I had desperately tried to hide from my wife was now plainly exposed to all. The initial x-rays showed that as a result of the injury to my foot, my heel bone had cracked and toxic gas had begun to seep up into my ankle. Because there is very little muscle in the foot, there was virtually no way to repair my heal. I needed to decide if I wanted to proceed with a below-knee amputation of my left foot. Waiting may endanger my entire leg or worse, my life. *Will I ever be able to drive again?"* was my weird first thought.

"Do you drive a stick?" my surgeon half jokingly asked.

"No," I replied, very seriously.

"Mr. Lyons, most amputees, after adjusting to their prosthetic, can resume almost all the activities that they experienced prior to their amputation. It will be a long journey, but you can do it. You are still young and have the right attitude." With those encouraging words, I looked at my wife, my podiatrist, my surgeon, and my pastor who had now joined the body of worried observers and said, "Let's do this, cut off my leg."

Three days and two surgeries later, I woke up laying on a cold operating room gurney after what felt like a deep coma like sleep. Disoriented, I thought that this must have all surely been a dream. I must have dreamed that I cut my foot in a freak accident involving my favorite snow boots. I must have dreamed that I was stupid enough to wait four weeks before having a medical professional look at the wound. I must have dreamed that this little cut resulted in the amputation of my left foot below my knee. This dream sequence was abruptly interrupted by stark reality as I looked down and only saw one tent at the foot of my bed where two healthy legs leave the specific indenture of two impressions, two tents. This was now a fact. I was newly disabled; permanently disabled. As I waited to be transported to my hospital room, I silently wondered what life held for a black, middle-aged amputee in job transition. Would I walk again? Would I work again? Did I have anything left to offer? I quickly worked to fight back these negative thoughts and combat them with affirmations of faith and hope.

"I was built for this fight!" I thought! *"Everything in my life has prepared me for this moment,"* I assured myself. And though I was cold, groggy, hungry, and a little afraid, this initial pep talk was the basis for my self-talk soundtrack. Four phrases flashed on and off in my mind the way a marquee lights up a dimly lit boulevard, *"Be more thankful, be more inquisitive, be more in the moment, be more prepared."* These were the first thoughts that went through my mind and if this was the syllabus, my goal was to learn the lesson as quickly as possible.

A Prayer for Pee

The first step toward my come back was the transfer from the hospital to a rehab facility. But before I could leave the hospital, I had to pass urine under my own power. After an operation, the staff keeps a strict record of how much urine you produce. "Produce" is the operative word, as urine can quickly become like taxes. Everyone is familiar with the Chris Rock joke that says, "You don't have to pay taxes, the government 'takes' taxes!" Well, when you don't make urine in a hospital they *take* urine as well! As many of you know, this is done using a catheter. During my stay, I was introduced to the catheter on two occasions. All I remember is the nurse removing the catheter from its sterile container and me screaming like a stuck pig. I should have known that the pain would be intense as Elaine got really quiet and demure, not her normal posture, and looked the other way when the procedure began. It is like Elaine and the nurse knew that within seconds of applying this apparatus to my penis, I would be crying like a little b——. After that, my new goal in life was to never, ever feel the intense pain and burn of a catheter again.

"By the time I come back, Mr. Lyons, you either have to produce urine or we will use a catheter to get it," the nurse said. I knew I needed divine intervention. At just that moment, the Grace Chaplain wandered into my room to see if I needed anything. At Grace, not only did they have a staff of chaplains, they also had daily prayer at eight twenty-five each morning and scripture strategically posted on the walls around the complex. They were committed to the mission of, "We bring to life the healing ministry of Jesus through our compassionate care and exceptional service." I wanted to give this specific chaplain an opportunity to put the mission into action! I told him of my challenge faced with the task of producing urine or the prospect of a catheter. I told him that I needed him to pray for me to produce my own urine. I needed a "prayer for pee." Initially, he seemed curious and a bit perplexed, but then he shook off any hesitancy, took my hand, and recited a wonderful prayer asking for God's grace and mercy in the form of urine. I am not sure of his exact words, but right after he left, I grabbed the bedside urinal and pee began to flow like a river. God will truly meet you at the point of your needs! Lying in bed with my manhood in one hand and a plastic urinal in the other, I don't believe that I have ever praised God before like I did that afternoon at Grace. I never saw that chaplain again but I hope he knows that he has a direct line to God and I wish that his "prayer for pee" could make him a candidate for canonization. It was truly a miracle!

Grace Rehab

I had high hopes for the progress that I would experience during my time at Grace Rehab. This campus was clean and quiet and filled with people who needed to learn how to walk again due to an amputation. I must have passed this place a million times but never really knew what happened there.

I imagined the place to be like some type of secret lair, like in superhero movies, dedicated to the purpose of putting injured superheroes back together again. At fifty-one years old, I was one of the younger, fitter residents, at least by the looks of things. I had plenty of time to observe all my fellow residents during the parade of the bruised and broken that took place every day before each meal. Each day, the staff would line up an army of wounded and march us into the dining room. Some of us had help moving our wheelchairs down the hallway and some of us gently rolled ourselves toward the community room with the large windows at the front of the center. Inch by inch, each wheelchair would move toward the cafeteria, get our meals, and wheel to an open table to eat our meal. Once done ordering your food, staff gladly took your tray to a table of your choosing. Feeling lonely and dejected, I always chose a table by the window, taking advantage of the only exposure to the sun I would experience all day. Food for me was a challenge as my vegetarian diet wrecked the plans of the facility's dietitian.

"Do you eat fish?" she asked.

"Nope, nothing with parents," I responded.

This phrase seemed to make an impression on the listener and eliminate any further discussion regarding my eating plan. Everyone made a point of telling me that I needed to have a high-protein diet so my residual limb would heal. This was scary as my gastrointestinal issues made traditional alternative sources of protein like beans, seeds, and milk-based supplements difficult for me to digest. Managing my diet from this point on would become more complex and multiple health issues made deciding what to eat more difficult.

Wheelchair-bound individuals have to adopt a number of new skills to manage their daily tasks. The more skills you add, the higher your level of independence. The higher the level of independence, the higher the quality of life you could enjoy. Until my residual limb healed and I could be fitted for a prosthesis, I was wheelchair bound and needed to master as many of these skills as possible. I had a great deal of hesitation because, up until my incident, I considered my left leg to be my "good leg." It was the leg I favored when going up stairs one at a time. It was the leg I used to pivot on and off of the elliptical. It was the leg I used to board a plane all those years while ascending the Jetway. Now it was the "weak leg" that needed metal and plastic to help me do something I had done effortlessly my entire life. It was also the leg that needed healing before we could even begin the rebuilding process.

The first skill I needed to master was transferring. This was the process of using my body weight to slide from my bed to my wheelchair. Initially using a slide board apparatus to assist in this process, being able to transfer properly would directly determine how much freedom I experienced on a daily basis. Could I transfer from my bed to my wheelchair? Could I transfer from my wheelchair to my bedside commode? What about from the bedside commode, back to the wheelchair then back to the bed? These transfer skills would outline how I started out each day. There were other transfer skills I had to master as well. A few times a week, I would need to transfer to the shower chair. I must admit that this scared me most of all as the shower chair on the wet floor presented a lot of opportunities for slips and falls to happen. Once in a shower chair, cleaning yourself as an amputee was quite the adventure as well; scrubbing your body parts while maintaining your balance so that you don't fall on the floor during the middle of your shower. In the back of my mind, I could visualize those commercials where the elderly woman slips in the shower and cannot get up; water running down her face from the shower head. I wanted to avoid becoming "that guy" but what I came to realize was falling was part of the journey. I would learn this quickly as the staff at Grace Rehab dropped me several times.

A good rehab facility is stocked with dozens of caring health professionals. This includes doctors, RNs, aides, therapists, and other staff that assists with the daily care of the residents. Their goal was to effectively manage their checklist of accountabilities that provided for your care. The doctors and RNs managed medicine, aides managed food and transport, and therapists managed life skills. Your time with therapists was most intense and they normally knew more about your day-to-day progress than the other health professionals. All these professionals had the same issue; too many patients and not enough time. The shuffling of professionals in and out of your case complicated the day-to-day interactions as well. I found myself frustrated as I had to tell my story over and over again to every professional. Sometimes, it felt like I was telling the story just to satisfy their curiosity. I always wanted to ask them, "Have you read my file? Do you even know who I am? My name is Darren Lyons, in February of 2017, I had an injury to my left foot. Due to my negligence, it did not heal properly, resulting in a below-knee amputation of my left leg. Yes, I am a diabetic. Yes, I have kidney disease."

I told that story to every doctor, therapist, nurse, and technician, in Oklahoma City! If I had I been smart, I would have put the story on flash cards and set it to music much like those Facebook presentations that were popular back in the day. Being a jerk, however, would not have endeared me to the well-meaning staff. I am sure that this ritual was necessary both for accurate medical assessments of the practitioner as well as self-awareness. This is especially true for an amputee as you need to always be aware of the fact that you no longer had your limb so that you can prevent falls. This process was exhausting, however, as every time I retold my story, it dragged me back to the time and place of injury. This retelling of the facts kept me in anger and regret, prompting me to reask the questions that hover in the back of the mind of all amputees: "Why me?" "Why was

I not smart enough to avoid this?" "Is my life ever going to be the same?" I guess you have to deal with these questions at some point but not on a daily basis. I hated talking about what happened in the past to get me to this position. Don't get me wrong, I did not mind sharing with people my struggle and how they could avoid a similar path. As a matter of fact, it felt good to be used as a tool to warn people about the pitfalls of not managing your blood pressure, blood sugar, and the like. What I had no interest in doing was waxing on and on regarding my condition and my treatment, especially, when there was no good news to share. That is why I struggled with having people visiting me. People really wanted the details of your condition, often out of pure concern for you but sometimes so they would not fall into a similar state. Neither of these were bad reasons to have these conversations as any concern for your physical condition is good. But this guard I kept up repelled people from my hospital room and, admittedly, made my hospital stays longer and lonelier.

In the back of the rehab facility, there was a large gym where the therapy for the residents took place. This hardwood floor room housed the apparatus used to restore each superhero back to their former glory. I remember the words spoken to me by the surgeon, "Someone with a prosthetic should be able to do the same things they did prior to their amputation." My first task was learning how to stand on my right leg. I did a pretty good job of using the slide board to transfer from place to place, but strengthening my right leg to support my body weight was a whole new ball game. Not only would this skill add to my current independence as an amputee, but the ability to stand on my right leg would directly determine the strength and flexibility I would need when I received my prosthetic.

The physical therapist worked on both my legs to help them regain strength in order to lift my body from the wheelchair to a standing position. The occupational therapist worked on my upper body so that my arms could adequately support my legs in rising from my wheelchair to a full stand. Each also schooled me on the technique of getting to the edge of the chair, bending low, and shifting my weight from my arms to legs properly to facilitate this. Things were going pretty well too as the therapist helped me stand up a few times using the parallel bars and a special mat in the gym. That's when the bedside fall incident happened and pretty much ended the standing routine. It is funny that falling is the thing you feared the most and yet it was the condition you most needed to face and overcome. I would spend my fifty-first birthday at Grace Rehab Hospital, propped up in my wheelchair. As I enjoyed some gifts and a few visitors, I could not help but reflect on how much my life had changed in one year.

In March of 2016, at this same time, I was enjoying a fete that rivaled any I had experienced. I was a corporate executive making well into the six figures. Now I was an unemployed amputee struggling with how to stand on one leg. Look how the mighty had fallen!

Diarrhea

Not being able to stand and walk is certainly a downer. Constant diarrhea is devastating! During my stay at Grace Rehab, I experienced the worst diarrhea of my life. My diabetes-related gastrointestinal tract issues made me a candidate for this complication but C. diff raised it to a new level. For those of you that are not familiar with this condition, Clostridium difficile, or C. diff, is a bacterium that can cause symptoms ranging from diarrhea to life-threatening inflammation of the colon. Illness from C. difficile most commonly affects older adults in hospitals or in long-term care facilities and typically occurs after use of antibiotic medications. The antibiotic vancomycin, along with my extended hospital stays, greatly increased the possibility of me catching the infection. After each meal, as well as each night, I had constant diarrhea. There is nothing as discouraging as waking up in a pool of your own feces. And feces gets everywhere—on your bed, on your hands, on your wheelchair, on your face.

Elaine repeatedly telling me that I missed a spot or cleaning up after me became a daily point of contentment. My two wheelchairs had dung stains dripping down the back of each and into the motor of the electric chair. My sneakers had dried poop on them that we can never remove. Hand sanitizer, wipes, and disinfectant became the tools of my travel kit. That scenario would repeat itself for months as I tried to shake this condition. My diarrhea left me lacking the confidence and desire to even slide from my bed to my chair as I joined the parade of the wounded. In addition to this, C. diff kind of gave you a scarlet letter in the facility as a large warning was placed on your room door and now every person who entered the room had to wear a mask, gloves, and gown upon entering.

In addition to the diarrhea, C. diff left me dizzy, gave me a fever, and zapped my energy. What made this infection even more frustrating is that the prescription for the cure was the same as the cause; more vancomycin! No one seemed to find it odd that this "life-saving drug" that gave me intense diarrhea, caused my food to taste weird, and left me hoarse was also my path back to health. Tapering me off the drug over an eight-week period was the determined course of action. If that did not work, a more invasive procedure was suggested; a fecal transplant. This is a procedure where they take the fecal matter of a healthy twenty-year-old and implant it in the colon of the C. diff patient. The prognosis was that I would have this condition well into my transition home. C. diff would complicate my care and reduce my quality of life for the foreseeable future. This meant that my wife would have the task of nightly helping me clean up after multiple diarrhea episodes. One night after a particularly violent, exhausting night of multiple episodes of repeated diarrhea, my wife just stood by my bedside and cried over my dehydrated body. Before C. diff, I defined love using the same general terms as most people: devotion, trust, acceptance, and sacrifice. Post C. diff, I now know what real love is; your partner's willingness to wake up several times a night and help you clean up your shat. Elaine had that "C.-diff kind of love" for me.

Sabolitch

T hree months after my amputation, I made my first trip to the company that would create my prosthetic leg, Scott Sabolitch. A family-run business founded in the mid-forties, Sabolitch was a world-class organization that just happened to be twenty minutes from my house. I considered it to be divine intervention; much like a cancer patient living in the shadow of the Mayo clinic. During my initial visit I met a paraplegic athlete from Los Angeles who traveled cross-country periodically to have his leg adjusted for competition. Many people traveled from all across the world to have their legs, arms, and hands created and adjusted by the staff at Sabolitch. The company you select for this procedure would be a decision that impacted your quality of life indefinitely.

During my initial visit to my new prosthetist I knew that I was in the right place. The lobby of Sabolitch was a magical place! As I sat waiting for my appointment, I was encouraged by the number of people walking back and forth with their prosthetic legs. Some, like me, had below-knee amputations which made this process less complex. Many of them, however, had above-knee amputations as well as double amputations. You would not have known that they were an amputee if they were not proudly displaying their mechanical leg beneath their cargo shorts. I sat there in amazement as they passed by, walking unassisted, and many without even a limp. I felt inspired and motivated that after my four fitting sessions I, too, would join the legion of new amputees with a fresh outlook on a new life.

Hanging from the center of the beautifully decorated lobby above the wall mounted fish tank was a five-foot crystal collage of a juggler. Sitting there, it occurred to me that a juggler was the perfect mascot for the life of an amputee. Everything now was a process. As an amputee, every move, no matter how simple, needed to be thought out in advance. If you had a doctor's appointment at 8:00 a.m., you had to get up at 6:00 a.m. in order to get to the bathroom to clean up prior to the visit. The night before, you consider your clothes; a change of underwear and your prosthetic leg needed to be within arm's reach of your bed when you wake up. How long will it take you to transfer from your chair to your car? Should you bring your slide board? Are your glasses nearby? What about your wallet? Does the doctor's office have a valet or will you need to transport yourself from the lot to the front door? Every scenario had dozens of possible twists and turns that needed to be juggled. The amputee focuses intensely on keeping the balls in the air while circumstances around him constantly change, adding new balls. Much like the primary goal of the juggler is to avoid dropping the balls as they are added, the primary goal of the amputee is to avoid falling. Dropping balls, much like falling, however, is how you become a better juggler and falling, I would learn, is necessary part of the journey of an amputee.

Donald was the prosthesis assigned with creating my new leg. His task was to create a mold that would support my residual limb so that I would have gait and balance to walk either with a walker or unassisted. As he explained the process to me, I could not help but get excited about the possibilities.

"Darren, after your surgeon gives us the okay, we will schedule a series of appointments for you. During the first, we will create a mold to fit your residual limb. That next week we will complete your initial fitting and you will stand up at the parallel bars. I will be constantly making adjustments to the joints to ensure we have the proper fit. We will repeat that process two or three more times and then I will let you take home your new leg."

Donald conveyed the type of easy confidence and vision that made all this seem possible. During our first fitting visit, I adapted to my new limb like a fish to water, strapping on my new leg and immediately standing up with the help of the parallel bars. Empowered and encouraged, I thought to myself, *"As long as these parallel bars magically appear every where I go, then I would be fine."*

This scenario repeated itself during my second visit, once again, strapping on my leg, and standing with the help of the parallel bars. This time, I strutted up and down the length of the room, performing what could best be described as A Temptations or Jackson 5 move. Much to the delight of my daughter and granddaughter, and to the horror of Donald, I executed several moves requiring fancy footwork as Donald attempted to make the adjustments necessary to my leg. With two fittings to go, I was gaining the type of confidence necessary to be an active amputee.

"Darren, let's do one more fitting and see if you may be ready to take home your leg after that!" It was what I longed to hear. Finally, there was something in this process moving ahead of schedule and not behind. If I could get my new leg in July, then this health scare would have been a speed bump in my life only slowing me down, not stopping me. Once again, my self-talk track betrayed me. During my third visit I struggled to even stand up on my prosthetic leg. Winded and weak, there was no repeat performance of the Temptations moves I displayed during the prior visit.

"It looks like you have been gaining some weight Darren," Donald commented. "Have you made any changes to your diet?"

A couple of weeks prior to my first fitting, I gave in and began eating meat for the first time in seven years. My wound was healing slowly and everyone said that I needed to be on a high-protein diet to facilitate the healing of my wound. Desperately, I turned to chicken, beef, and fish to give me that additional protein. My body did not respond well to this as I began to accumulate massive amounts of fluid on my left side and in my legs. My clothes no longer fit as, all told, I gained back ninety of the two hundred pounds I lost due to my vegetarian life style. In addition to this, the extra fluid made it difficult for me to get out of bed. The process of sitting up and trans-ferring to my wheelchair that once took fifteen minutes, now took two to three times as long.

The biggest disappointment came during my fourth fitting visit to Sabolitch. After another failed attempt of getting up on my leg,

Donald checked my temperature only to discover that I was running a high fever. "Maybe a virus would explain why you are having trouble getting up on your leg," Donald wondered aloud. My wife and I immediately made an appointment with my primary care physician to determine the cause of my infection. After a chest x-ray, I was sent to a cardiologist to get his expert opinion.

After a long wait and a quick exam, the cardiologist asked, "Mr. Lyons, how do you feel?"

"I feel fine, with the exception of my amputation, of course."

"Mr. Lyons, after examining you, I believe that you have a blockage in your aorta that is resulting in repository issues like wheezing, inability to sleeping on your back, and general weakness. I believe that it is also contributing to your weight gain along with your falling kidneys. I believe that your nephrologist has given you a best-case scenario regarding your kidneys, as diuretics alone will not get rid of your excess fluid. In my opinion, we need to perform an angiogram on you to determine the best course of action for your heart. The only problem is that the heart and the kidney are often in conflict with each other. A cure for one can damage the progress of the other. The heart takes precedence but I will let you and your nephrologist coordinate the next course of action. I will see you in a couple of weeks."

The doctor had been so cold and matter-of-fact about my condition that it left Elaine and I breathless. My heart sank as Elaine wheeled me into the hallway of the medical center. As she excused herself and went into the public bathroom to cry, I never felt so alone and hopeless. Just a few weeks ago, I seemed to be close to my breakthrough. Now, this additional bad news would further complicate my healing process. For the first time, I wondered, *Can I really make it back from this? I am a fifty-one-year-old man! What would the rest of my life look like?*

As we left the hospital, I couldn't help but think that everything I had worked for and every dream I ever had was now truly in jeopardy. With each disappointing prognosis hope was fading fast. Unfortunately the summer of 2017 would be a new low, pulling the arrow further and further back, making a come back more difficult and less likely.

Back at Home

A myriad of conditions conspired against me waging an effective come back. My effort to walk on my new leg was hampered by the amount of fluid I had gained. Reducing my fluid was made more difficult due to my now stage five kidney failure and a weakened heart. If I did not have a doctor's appointment, most days I laid in bed till noon, mustering up the strength to sit up in bed, and transfer to my electric wheelchair. Donated to me, the electric chair got me around the house better but robbed me of a daily work-out of my arms and legs provided by the manual wheelchair. I wish someone had warned me of this phenomena prior to making the transition.

Each day it was the same routine. Five minutes to move my body to sit up straight in bed. Another fifteen minutes to slide from my bed to the electric chair. Then I would untether the electric chair and ride a short distance to the bedside commode in the bathroom. Once completely finishing that process would go to the sink to wash hands and face and try to brush the taste of vancomycin from my mouth. The chair was only graded to hold someone approximately three hundred pounds. My new fluid gain had me tipping the scale at just above that. In addition to this, my legs swelled during the day, making it impossible to sit up straight much longer than six or seven hours a day. I would split this time between my office on my computer and playing Wii with my daughter and grandson. By the end of the day, the swelling would leave the electric wheelchair straining to transport me from my office back to my bedroom. To facilitate my movement, I used a blue resistance band. I would wrap this band around my left leg and suspend it so that it would not drag the ground as I transported back to the room. I would then use the band to help me safely get my legs back on the bed.

When I did leave the house, it was normally my oldest daughter charged with transporting me to my appointments. Although we were at war in the house, my daughter was dutiful as she assisted me in transferring from my chair to the car, putting my chair in the trunk, and then assisting me when I arrived at the doctor's office. Some days, she brought my grandchildren along with us and this only added to the fun. Some of my best memories of that summer were when following an appointment we would stop by a park or a playground. Arielle would take the children out to play and I would roll the window down and watch attentively from the car. Some of the lowest moments happened during that summer as well as there were three occasions where paramedics had to be called to scrape me off the bathroom, living room, and garage floor.

As I said before, falling was part of the process. Each fall gave you new information on how to slide, how not to lean against your body, and how to use your arms to assist your legs in moving from your wheelchair to a couch. My daughter shared many of these learning experiences with me that summer. The worst being a visit to a rehab facility downtown. My goal was to have them teach me how to use my prosthetic leg. My insurance company would only pay for a few more therapy sessions so I needed to find a company that could help me maximize my last few visits. As we went into the therapy gym, my daughter dutifully carried my prosthetic leg behind me as I wheeled in. I did not wear my leg much as the extra fluid made it uncomfortable to put on and nearly impossible to use. The therapist had me put on my leg and lay on a large mat to assess my flexibility and range of motion.

Her assessment was grim, "It is going to take you at least a dozen sessions or so to gain any flexibility using this leg. Your strength in both appendages seem to be compromised. Plus, there appears to be a large cut on the back of your knee of your residual limb. You are going to need to get that checked out by wound care immediately to insure that you do not get an infection."

After getting back into the car, Arielle shut the door and broke down in tears. My illness had now taken a profound toll on her. "Don't cry for me," I said defiantly. But I guess I could not blame her. I had met Arielle when she was eleven years old, moved her into my house in Tampa, and helped her transfer to Oklahoma City. She had lived under my roof for more than half of her life and now she was watching her "father" deteriorate in front of her eyes.

Home Health Care

One of the most uncomfortable parts of recovery was home health care. Having people visit your home in such an intimate setting for such an intimate purpose, like assessing your health or treating your wounds, can lead to some very awkward moments. Instantly, all your stuff is on display for this stranger to see. Three times a week, during each visit, your life would be on display. Did you all wash the dishes? Clean the kitchen? Is the laundry still on the couch? Books on the floor? You know we need to clean all that up and the house can't look the same as the last time the nurse visited!

After your initial assessment, you were ready for your regularly scheduled visits. As awkward as this arrangement was for you, a good home health care professional had the ability to normalize the visit.

"Good morning, Mr. Lyons, I am Alicia, your occupational therapist. I am here to assist you in your ability to care for yourself in your home. Let's see you transfer from your bed to your chair and wash your face."

This attractive, midforties white woman seemed oblivious to the fact that she was in the middle of my master bedroom, with her hand on my bedside commode and the only thing standing between my manhood being fully exposed was this thin, gray bedsheet. Obediently, after covering myself properly, I used my sliding board to transfer from my bed to my wheelchair. Sitting in front of the mirror, I was looking at my own face for what felt to be the first time in weeks. Swollen and now sporting a full beard.

I rubbed my face and said, "I used to be a pretty sharp-looking guy back in the day, Alicia."

"Why, you still are, Mr. Lyons!" she replied. "Do you want to try and brush your teeth and wash your face?"

"Sure." I said to Alicia as these sounded like the most novel ideas ever suggested to a patient.

"We have twenty minutes left, Mr. Lyons, what else would you like to accomplish today?" As I rummaged through the drawers beneath my vanity sink, I found my old hair clippers and some coconut oil. After looking closer, I found my guides and prepared my clippers for duty. It felt liberating as I began to cut my hair and beard. It was like using a shear to remove weeks of worry and layers of pain from my face and head. Under this accumulation of time and illness presenting itself as gray-and-black follicles was the face of a fifty-one-year-old, eager to get back his life.

Alicia would visit three times a week for the next couple of months. During that time, we would swap stories about our grown children and how their presence disrupted the normal order of our households. We would share our philosophies with each other on raising teenagers, buying first cars, and watching them attend their first proms. We would share many first, like Alicia helping me take my first real shower in five months. It was a milestone moment as Alicia, strong, shapely, but tiny, helped me transfer from my chair to the medical shower chair my wife had ordered for me. Always a process, we meticulously covered Ralphie (the nick name we gave my residual limb) and placed my good foot, still in a sneaker, into the tub. With Alicia's help, I used my arms to grab onto the shower chair, lift up, and manipulate my bottom into the shower chair. Then I dragged my bad leg into the other side of the chair, safely in the shower.

"This would be much easier if I had a left leg!" I jokingly told Alicia. She handed me the handheld shower head, closed the curtain and told me to call her when I was done. I looked around and grabbed my favorite shower gel, Mango and Peach Aromatherapy. Rubbing the lotion into my face and hair, I let the water gently wash away my worries and fears, at least temporarily. I remember a friend who was a cancer survivor once telling me about the therapeutic, restorative power of her first shower after her cancer surgery. Never has a truer statement been made as I was now feeling this first hand.

If my time with my occupational therapist was intimate, quiet, and reflective my time with my wound care nurse was the opposite. Tabitha visited three times a week, midmorning, with the job of assessing and changing the wound on my left leg in preparation for my new prosthetic limb. Tabitha was a single mother in her mid-thirties/early forties who had been a home health professional for a decade or so. More loud and bombastic than Alicia, we seemed to get off on the wrong foot, so to speak, during our first visit. Tabitha's appearance on our stoop caught my wife and I off guard as Elaine answered the door in her blue bath towel.

"Come on in, Tabitha, Darren is right back here in the bedroom." Tabitha looked as if she was on another planet as she carefully squeezed by Elaine to assess my leg. "I am sorry that I am still in my bathrobe, Tabitha, I am just trying to get out of here for work," Elaine said. Tabitha looked at Elaine as if she had a third head as she whipped out her blood pressure cuff and thermometer to begin her assessment. I laid there literally paralyzed as I tried not to lock eyes with Elaine. Tabitha whipped out her checklist, quickly made her assessment, and began to pack up her belongings. "We will change your wound three times a week for the next three weeks before making future assessments. I will also apply silver and santyl to the wound based on the assessment. This is my number should you need anything in between visits. Elaine, do you have any questions?" Tabitha asked my wife, looking her in the eye for the first time since Elaine initially let her in the door.

"No, no questions," Elaine replied. And as quickly, as Tabitha had appeared, she was gone. Over time, Tabitha's visits would become less and less awkward as we moved my time with her from the confines of my bedroom to the open air of the living room. CNN constantly in the background seemed to lighten the mood, along with the presence of my granddaughter, distracting us from the uncomfortable intimacy of a stranger gently rubbing your leg with oil as she wrapped and unwrapped the remains of the recently-amputated limb. Unfortunately, Tabitha's best efforts, and her increasingly pleasant ways, could not help my healing. My diabetes and a low-protein diet made my healing akin to the pace of a death march; healing was slow and I would eventually have to go to the Grace Wound Care Clinic to experience complete healing.

The Grace Wound Care Clinic was one of those hospital services that was difficult to start. I waited two weeks to get an appointment with the unit. Their receptionist staff protected their calendar religiously. Once you got on the calendar, however, you were in their rotation for what seemed like eternity. Maybe it is just the nature of wound care but everything about it denoted process and time. This step was the culmination of my monthly visits to my surgeon who originally performed my amputation. For three months, I went to his office only to have him tell me that we needed more time for my wound to heal before we could proceed with the prosthetic limb process. For three months I had humped up to my orthopedic surgeon's office, only to have him tell me the same chapter and verse, "The healing is no worse than before," and "We just need more time for the surface of the leg to toughen up."

He would always suggest that I go to wound care, but I rebuffed the thought as too expensive and just another hurdle in this gauntlet of steps that I had to take on this journey. It was not until after home wound care stalled that I was open to this option. I had imagined that the lobby of the wound care clinic would be filled with literally, well, the walking wounded. I was pleasantly surprised to find that entering and exiting the clinic was a pretty simple procedure. When you arrive in the exam room you quickly transfer from your wheelchair to a large recliner.

"Once you get in this, the chair is pretty comfortable, Mr. Lyons," the wound care nurse stated.

She was right as my body effortlessly slipped into the oversized recliner. The nurses in wound care always offered you the best indication of your progress. Weekly, they got the first look at your wound, sans Band-Aid, often snapping a picture of it, comparing it to the previous picture on file. After the picture they whip out tape and measured the length, depth and width of the wound, comparing it to prior measurements. Only after this would the actual wound Doctor come in, debride the wound and make any changes, if necessary to the treatment. As I stated before, wound healing was a slow, iterative process measured in weeks not days. Because it was the dog days of summer Arielle and the grandkids attended many of my wound care appointments. Every week they would watch me transfer from my wheelchair to the large recliner, signaling the beginning of each visit. We were quite a show for the staff, parading through the lobby each week to attend my appointments. It was in a race against time as the swelling on my heart, legs, and lungs were making this transfer increasingly more difficult. I was gaining weight, primarily due to adding meat back into my diet. Everyone was on me about needing a high-protein diet to facilitate the healing of my limb. I had heard this since leaving the rehab facility: "You need protein for your wound to heal and it is going to be difficult to get enough protein with your plant-based diet."

The protein shakes and other milk-based products did not make my digestive system happy. For the first time in seven and a half years, I had started eating meat again. Initially, it was just fish, but then I eventually gave in and included chicken and beef as part of my daily diet. It was a decision I grew to regret as my weight exploded. After six weeks of eating meat, I once again dismissed it from my diet. It had been a great mistake as my weight gain and the deterioration of my kidneys seemed to correspond with that habit. My wound did heal enough for me to finish my fitting for my prosthetic leg but at what costs to my overall health? A health professional once told me that they had never seen anyone die due to a lack of protein but had seen many people die due to heart disease. That statement sums up what I feel about my personal consumption of meat.

Paul was the miracle worker of the group. As my physical therapist, my progress would be most closely measured by the results of the time we spent together. Of West Indian descent, Paul's accent reminded me of all the kind Jamaicans I had met at my church over the years. An OU alumnus, Paul had built a good life here in Oklahoma, putting his own kids through school.

"Mr. Lyons, you have been down for a long time. My primary goal will be to strengthen your legs in preparation for your prosthetic. We will do a series of calisthenics and stretches which will improve your balance and gait. I will also give you a series of exercises using the free weights and a blue resistance band that you can do on your own."

It all sounded good in Paul's West Indian accent!

"As you get stronger, we will practice standing on your good leg. There is no better therapy for you than sitting and standing on that good leg, building up your muscles and restoring your strength."

"Paul, my left leg was my stronger limb before the amputation. Do you really think that it, alone, can support my entire body weight?"

"Why not, Mr. Lyons, why not?" Paul replied.

With that, Paul excused himself into my kitchen. "*I had not been in my kitchen in weeks,*" I thought to myself.

"You have a nice sink in your kitchen. During my next visit, we will wheel you up to your sink, have you get a good grip on the inside of it, and stand."

So you say Paul, so you say... I thought to myself.

I had what can only be described as a "man crush" on Paul. I anxiously anticipated his visits, texted back and forth with him to coordinate the next touch point; I even tried to look my best in front of him.

"Mr. Lyons, we are going to get your chair close to the sink and grab hold to each side with your right and left hand and try to stand. Slide up to the edge of your chair, place your hands flat on the arms of your chair, turn your good foot inward, bending low, and lean your body all the way forward. On your way up, let your body weight shift from your good leg to your left arm, grabbing the sink. That's it, lock that right leg, stand straight up!"

The instructions of a good therapist played over and over in your mind like a soundtrack. We were not successful in standing up every time, but over the next three weeks, Paul and I repeatedly practiced this process. He was a master juggler!

"I think I am going to walk again, Paul."

"Why not, Mr. Lyons, why not?"

Seizures

My entire world was now primarily confined to my master bedroom. Now that I had my prosthetic leg, there were fewer doctor visits and no visiting nurses and therapists from home health care. I was now at a crossroads as I had survived an amputation but the additional health issues, diabetes, heart disease, and kidney failure, collectively forced me into a decline that felt unescapable. I was circling the drain now, slowly. A very low quality of life and existing each day on very little interaction with any one. People tried to connect but recanting my illness over and repeatedly to different visitors kept me in the past and I desperately wanted to talk about the future, my hopes and dreams. I longed for normal conversations, casual, yet intentional. Besides Facebook and a few business connections, my only real contact with the outside world was through my wife, brother and father, my pastor and a few frat brothers.

During my illness, my wife continued to work for an agency that provided benefits for the elderly. Her job required that she travel within the state using a company car to visit her members, assessing their care needs, and arranging for supplies like bed pads, shower rods, bedside commodes, shower chairs, and other necessities that the elderly used to elevate their quality of life. Elaine's formal education and kind heart made her a natural for this work. In addition to this, being out in the field afforded her the flexibility to take me to many of my appointments in support of my recovery. Elaine leaving the house and her return home were the highlights of my day. It was especially rewarding when I did not have to interrupt her work day with a diarrhea episode.

One evening, Elaine was meeting an old friend from Tampa for dinner at Cracker Barrel. A southern, highway rest stop favorite, Cracker Barrel specialized in comfort foods and served breakfast all day. My wife was especially taken by their hash brown potato casserole le dish which was more of a desert than a vegetable. Rudy was passing through town on business so he and Elaine planned to meet and enjoy a late night pig out. When I woke up at 2:00 a.m., Elaine was sitting on the floor. Soaked in her own vomit. She was incoherent and stammered over her words. I immediately called Arielle and had her and her husband break into the bedroom door. Arielle called the paramedics and they rushed her off to the hospital for tests. When she returned home several hours later, they said that she was drunk and passed out when she got home. The only problem with this prognosis is that Elaine was a teetotaler at best and rarely drank outside the home. Plus, she had been hanging out with our good Seventh Day Adventist brother from our old church, hardly a drinking partner. Finally, they ate dinner at Cracker Barrel. People get full at Cracker Barrel, not drunk. The only coma that people go into at "The Barrel" was induced by carbohydrates, not liquor.

Two days later, I would wake up to Elaine's body violently shaking back and forth on her bed before flinging to the floor below. I once again had Arielle and her husband call the paramedics who rushed her to the hospital. After closer observation from a more skilled emergency room staff, it was determined that Elaine had suffered two Grand Mal seizures. Two years earlier, Elaine had survived brain surgery, having a softball-sized tumor removed from the front lobe of her brain. I remember that day vividly as twenty family members, friends, and church members met us in the waiting room that morning, in preparation for her surgery. Elaine was cool and reflective as she awaited this life-changing event. For two years, I had noticed a specific change in her demeanor and attitude. She would often drift off in the middle of conversation and quickly lose interest in anything I had to say. During my routine of back to back meetings, Elaine called and after a scheduled MRI her doctor received her results and immediately called less than 5 minutes after completing the scan. It was a tumor that had apparently been growing for over ten years. She was so cool with it and confident that she spent more time consoling me than worrying for herself. "We will have the surgery in 3 weeks", she calmly said. Those 3 weeks were like a blur to me as my eyes filled with tears any time someone mentioned her condition to me. She was like a Zen master, celebrating her birthday in advance of her surgery and thoughtfully making preparations for our life as a family just in case she was no longer herself after the procedure. Maybe it is childbirth or maybe it is a lifetime of caring for others, but women seem innately equipped for these types of life jarring circumstances compared to men. Elaine was a "G" through all of this; I was a mess. Elaine had recovered famously from her brain surgery. Three hours after the surgery, Elaine was on social media, sending messages to family and friends. As part of her recovery, Elaine daily took anti-seizure medication. A one -year milestone was the okay from the doctor to stop taking the anti-seizure meds if there were no issues. The stress of my illness along with our living conditions had brought on seizures that would further complicate our lives.

Elaine's seizures caused a number of problems for us as we tried to move forward. Now Elaine was considered an epileptic. This posed the danger of additional seizures and other brain-related issues. As an epileptic, by law, she could no longer drive and had to go six months without an episode to regain those driving privileges. This would make it impossible for Elaine to transport me back and forth to doctor's appointments and dialysis sessions. Without the ability to drive, Elaine would eventually lose her job as she no longer had the ability to visit her members in the field. Without a job, in time, we would lose the health insurance that we were relying upon for our care. The new seizure medication left Elaine confused, lethargic, and sapped her of her energy. For two weeks, she laid in bed nearly as long as I did each day trying to muster up the energy to return calls from concerned family members and her office.

In addition to all this, the new meds made her frustrated, argumentative, and just plain mean. I had always been drawn to Elaine's strong character and sweet disposition. When we were dating, she showered me with her beautiful smiles and compliments on my good looks and how I had given her a great quality of life. This was the opposite of that. Everything now was a debate—her care, my care, our home. Any comment regarding my health turned into a retracing of every bad decision I had ever made.

"At the beginning of our marriage, you promised to do something about your health! You lied to me!"

"But, honey, I did not lie to you, I lost over two hundred pounds. Who does that?"

"Yeah, but you did not do anything about your diabetes and your blood pressure," she would reply.

"Who knew that I would need to do more for my health than lose two hundred pounds?" I retorted.

This argument repeated itself over and over during my illness, especially during the weeks immediately following her taking her new seizure meds. The conversation was like attending your mother's funeral every single day. Elaine had been my "ride or die" partner for over sixteen years. Now, time with her was tough. As much as an amputee can hide, I avoided time with her and certainly ducked conversations. I could not apologize any more or any other variety of ways. I tried to weather the storm of her contempt with patience and understanding. Admittedly, these characteristics were not my strong suit.

Physical Transformation

My enlarged heart and failed kidneys put me back in the hospital on Halloween 2017. Over the next two days, I would have an angiogram to determine if there was any blockage in the blood vessels of my heart. If there was a blockage, they would open it up with a stent. After that procedure, the next team would place a catheter (not that type of catheter) in my chest so that I could begin dialysis. My nephrologist and I were hoping that we could put off dialysis for four to five more years but, unfortunately that was not the case. The swelling, especially on my left side, had gotten so bad that I was grossly disfigured and barely able to move.

The day after placing a stent in my blocked artery to address a 90 percent blockage, I began dialysis. This would first take place in the hospital prior to proceeding to an outpatient skilled nursing facility upon my release. Prior to my first session, I had swelled up to 335 pounds due to the excess fluid. Before my incident, I was tipping the scales at 250 or so. After two weeks of dialysis sessions, I was down to 225 pounds adding on to my original weight loss by twenty-five pounds. I would eventually get down to about 205 pounds which was a total loss of 260 pounds when compared to my highest recorded weight. This was total transformation as the staff commented on how my hospital bed was now swallowing me up and I was quickly shrinking. My middle knuckles, once flat and nondescript, now protruded from the side of each finger. My fingers were long and lean, resembling the "Cryptkeeper" and reminding me of the well-worn hands of my ninety-year-old grandfather, Bub. My hands, once swollen and nondescript, now displayed an impressive network of intersecting veins and bones that started at the knuckle and extended down through my now-skinny wrist. I would certainly need new bands for all my watches!

My arms, though certainly not cock diesel, now had the form and shape of someone participating in physical therapy. My wife described my shoulders as boney but for the first time, they were broader than my waist. My wife and I smiled as we noticed a rib cage and a hip bone for the first time. My face, which displayed chubby cheeks the majority of my life, now had angles, accented with the lines that indicate someone who has seen the world, overcome some adversity, and cried a few tears. It was all framed by a full black and gray beard giving my new look more definition. Friends had joked that I was no longer "Big D," I was now "S'medium D." Like the old folks used to say, I looked at my hands and they looked new. I looked at my feet and they did too. Elaine said I was handsome; all I knew was, for the first time since June, I could easily sit up in bed and easily slide to my chair. When I returned home, I would no longer have to be confined to my room for sixteen hours a day. Walking on my prosthetic could not be far behind!

> Broken, lost and confused
> How'd I even come to this
> A life that's in ruins
> Is there a rope that I can cling to
> Is there a way to make it through
> Can I stoop and build 'em up
> Can I stoop and build 'em up
> Can I stoop and build 'em up
> With worn-out tools

A Skilled Nursing Facility

T hey called it a "skilled nursing facility." But let's be real and call it what it was; a nursing home! That is the realization that I came to when the medics transported me to Diamond Care that Saturday evening. This arrangement was actually a bit of a Hail Mary pass thrown by my wife and my nephrologist, Dr. Neeravta. Because of my wife's recent two grand mal seizures, she was unable to drive for at least six months according to Oklahoma State Law. In addition to this, the side effects of her new seizure medications and their impact on her motor skills, memory, and energy left her temporarily unable to care for me. My wife and my doctor figured that if I was in a skilled nursing facility, I would at least have transportation to my dialysis sessions and my doctor's appointments. I would also have assistance in the self-care I needed as I continued to contend with my ever-increasing bowel issues. Caring for a loved one can be a drain on a relationship and my illness had certainly taken a toll on my marriage. A break from each other, though painful to consider, may actually do us some good. I know that her body needed the physical break and I needed the perspective that can only be gained by having intense alone time. I know that I had begun to get snappy with her and as she saw my life slipping away she began to snap right back.

But, this "skilled nursing facility" was a real-life nursing home! My only real nursing home experience was memories of the last years of my grandmother's life that was spent in the same type of place. For approximately three years, my active, vibrant maternal Grandmother went into steady decline, diminishing in physical stature, and mental capacity. I imagined that her nursing home bed was the platform used to resolve her final life issues as she lied in a catatonic state for months on end. I am not sure if it is the isolation or the sounds or the smells of a nursing home that lead to this type of decline. As I was rolled into my temporary home. I wondered if this soul-sucking environment would conspire to lead me to a similar fate. Although I was only fifty-one years old, as the medics pushed me to the last room on the left on the B hall, I saw my very existence slipping away. The undecorated room with a flat-screen TV and cinderblock walls gave you that cold institutional vibe unlike the natural warmth of the hospitals and rehab facilities that I had stayed in earlier in the year. The room was devoid of any niceties or amenities that a place a functioning member of the human race would call "normal." This was a different world.

Although clean and well-kept, my instincts told me that on the spectrum of "skilled nursing facilities" my temporary home was more Holiday Inn than Ritz-Carlton. If this health incident was a prize fight, then being sent to a "skilled nursing facility" was the equivalent of being on the receiving end of a haymaker. This punch, however, was fortified with the power of fear, the leverage of loneliness, and the impact of hopelessness. Make no mistake; having my foot amputated earlier that year was certainly the defining moment of this health incident. The experience of waking up for the first time and seeing only one impression of an appendage at the foot of your bed is a sobering and life-changing moment. A screaming slap in the face that your life will never be the same. But being wheeled into this nursing home for an indefinite stay had the potential to be a soul-sucking, unrecoverable blow. As the medics used the portable patient lift apparatus to transfer me from the stretcher to my 1980s era hospital bed, I decided at that moment that, "*I was not going out like this. I can't go out like this!*" The refrain of a sermon by TD Jakes immediately rang out in my consciousness. It shouted out to me to, "*Fight back, fight back! Fight the helplessness, fight the loneliness, and fight the fear.*" I instantly knew that I had to fight my way out of this condition or my ultimate demise would be inevitable.

The first person I met on my arrival was Grenada, the weekend supervising nurse for the facility. Grenada was probably in her mid-thirties and seemed pleasant enough and well-intended. The admitting supervisory administrative responsibilities threatened to overwhelm her as they seemed to be bolted on to the medical accountabilities of the Hall B nurse. To help manage this, she had what every medical professional I had met over the past ten months had. A checklist. I had learned that medical professionals were religiously dedicated to their checklists. The list, though often mental and not physical, ruled each patient interaction. I am sure that the checklist led to "efficient" exchanges but it often detracted from the human nature desperately needed by the patient during the first moments of their initial meeting. After confirming my name and date of birth, Grenada proceeded to the first item on her checklist.

"I need to ensure that you have no open wounds or breakage in your skin," Grenada told me. This was checklist for "Now, lie on your back, strip off your clothes, and put your legs in the air so I can check your genitals and butt for sores."

As I laid there, in the position much like a turtle lying on its' shell, feet dangling in the air, my first thought was, *Skilled nursing home, 1 point; my dignity, 0!*

"All clear," Grenada said. "That's what I like to see, no sores or breakage," My dignity may have whiffed in this instance but at least the skin around my groin stood strong when tested. I could clearly see this fight with the skilled nursing facility would be about the little wins.

I was actually feeling pretty good about passing Grenada's test when in walked the biggest, most frightening-looking nurse's aide on the planet. Easily standing over six feet tall, yellowed-eye, and blue-black, this aide singularly manifested all the fears that I had about nursing home personnel. I am not normally intimidated by someone's physical presence. All my life I had been a big, hefty guy. Let's face it, when I weighed over 450 pounds I never worried about being physically dominated by other people. But after losing well over two hundred pounds as a result of a seven-year vegetarian diet, I realized my heft was no longer startling or powerful. I was also adjusting to being a new amputee who depended on caregivers to push me around. As a man, this took a toll on my confidence to defend or even protect myself. The aide had not uttered a word; he just gave me an icy glare. I did not even know his name but I imagined that it was a multisyllable, guttural-sounding utterance, personifying a power moniker like Mustafa, Akbar, or God Emperor. Whatever his name was, I could tell he thought I was weak and pathetic and this perception of me left me feeling vulnerable and unsafe in this new environment.

With Granada looking on, God Emperor asked me if I had eaten and I said, "No, I had not." God Emperor then said that they had a tray with sandwiches of ham and turkey that could keep me until the next day. The kitchen had closed and the cooking staff had already left for the evening. As he showed me the tray I told God Emperor that I was a full vegetarian and meat actually made me sick to my stomach. In addition to this, I was a diabetic with a failing kidney and gastro issues, so, my diet had restrictions of sugar, sodium, potassium, and phosphate.

He looked at me with a hint of disgust and snatched the sandwiches back and simply said, "Sandwiches not for you."

"Great," I thought to myself. *"I am not only intimidated, but I am also starving."*

After the weekend dietician wrestled me up some peanut butter and a salad (no dressing or tomatoes), Grenada and God Emperor left me alone in my room. The remote for the flat-screen did not work and the facilities engineer, of course, was off-duty for the weekend. "Never start off your stay in a skilled nursing facility on the weekend," I thought silently. As I sat there, alone, dejected, and discouraged, I saw my prosthetic leg haphazardly propped up in the corner of the room on top of my personal effects. My wife and I nicked named my prosthetic leg Ralph Lauren, or Ralphie for short (Ralph Lauren was code for residual limb.) Although I got my leg in August, I had not spent any real time using it. As a matter of fact, my failing kidney caused me to gain nearly ninety pounds of fluid since my amputation. This fluid gain made it impossible for me to even stand up on my leg under my own power. I had not demonstrated the strength or the confidence to even try and stand up without the assistance of the two parallel bars at the rehab facility. Desperation, however, is a powerful motivator, and my introduction to a skilled nursing facility certainly filled me with desperation. With no distractions, I heard the refrain of that sermon in my mind once again admonishing me to "Fight, fight, fight." With that talk track cutting through the silence of my room, I got dressed, transferred from my bed to my wheelchair, and rolled across the room to retrieve my prosthetic limb. I rolled back across the room and positioned my chair facing the bed. After strapping on Ralphie, I took a deep breath, leaned forward and I stood on my leg under my own strength for the very first time. As I stood there with the chair behind me, and the bed in front of me in case I fell, I thought, *"I might make it through this. I might make it back to life."*

On that Monday morning, I began to meet the medical staff that would play a critical role in my recovery. If this Hail Mary was going to work, I had to get the most out of my stay in the facility. They didn't know it but they were going to get the most engaged, motivated patient they had ever come across. I was determined to fight against my natural desire to be passive about my health; asking questions, communicating concern, and articulating thoughts and feelings. A couple of years ago, I read a book called, *Black Man in a White Coat* by Damon Tweedy. In this book, he goes on at length at how race, age, and social economic status shapes the perception of medical personnel and impacts the level and quality of care that you receive. He goes on to state that medical professionals could not help these perceptions as they were ingrained in them due to years of interactions with patients with specific demographics.

As a fifty-one-year-old African American amputee with diabetes, a failing kidney, and congestive heart failure, I feared that they would write me off as a sad case and not match my level of urgency to make a comeback to a full recovery. In addition to this, I had no idea how long my insurance company would allow me to recover in the skilled nursing facility. I felt there was an internal clock counting down my every second at Diamond Care. With this in mind, I was determined to be my most articulate when speaking with the medical staff. I also attempted to look my best each day. Due to my weight loss, I was swimming in my clothes, but I ensured that my chosen wardrobe included popular labels when at all possible. Finally, I attempted to engage the staff at every turn and all the staff in pleasant conversation. I chitchatted with the nurses, the therapists, the receptionists, the custodial staff and the other patients.

I figured, *If they liked me, they would give me the highest level of care that they could offer.* My dress, my words, and my attitude would act as a safeguard against negative perceptions and an accelerator of my recovery. The staff was going to get the Denzel Washington version of Darren; charming, upbeat, and positive.

My initial impression of the Diamond Care staff was positive. Everyone conducted themselves in a very caring and professional manner. As I stated previously, I was suspicious of everyone I encountered but that suspicion slowly dissipated as I interacted with the medical professionals. I was pleasantly surprised by the patience demonstrated by the physician's assistant as he listened to me chronicle my health history. I gave him the type of detail that left no question that I needed the healing hands of the skilled nursing facility. I was practicing telling the story of my medical demise; going on at length about my amputation in February, congestive heart failure in August, kidney failure in September, and the subsequent medical procedures in October that addressed the chronic issues. These procedures included an angioplasty and dialysis. I forgot to even mention the colonoscopy performed on me in July to address my gastrointestinal condition. He was both attentive and engaged as he logged our conversation; managed by his checklist, of course.

"He seems competent," I surprisingly thought to myself as he left the room for his next patient.

The staff dietician stopped by to get a look at me and have a conversation.

I said "Take a look at me," because maintaining a vegetarian diet in the land of beef and barbecue which, in Oklahoma, seemed to catch everyone by surprise. Also, I did not really have that "lean, healthy look" possessed by most vegetarians. Although my plant-based lifestyle significantly contributed to my 250-pound weight loss, I still looked like I was a wing and a biscuit away from a heart-stopping binge at Church's Chicken or Popeyes. In addition to this, amputees are encouraged to adopt a high-protein diet as it helps your wounds to heal. Getting enough protein is a challenge for a vegetarian on the outside, let alone a vegetarian in a skilled nursing facility. My diet was also complicated by kidney failure, diabetes, GI issues, and congestive heart failure. Each condition required a distinct, often conflicting restriction. Diabetes required that you limit your sugar intake, kidney disease demanded that I watch my sodium, potassium and phosphorus. My gastrointestinal issues required that I avoid raw vegetables and fruit, wheat, beans, and seeds. In essence, what I needed was a high protein, low sugar, low sodium, low potassium, and low phosphorus meal plan. I was confident that the dietician would try to convince me to eat meat for the good of my amputation. Medical professionals seemed to admire my choice of a plant-based diet but always seems to suggest that I include "some meat" in my diet. Meat was not an option for me as I had fallen down this rabbit hole before. After over seven years of strictly avoiding meat, I decided to include chicken, fish, and some beef in my daily meal plan.

For six weeks, I wheeled into my kitchen and breaded or broiled chicken wings, chicken breast, and chicken legs. For one meal a day, I ate as much flesh as I could take. I convinced myself that "eating this chicken was a key to my healing!" The stories we tell ourselves!

That next month, I was diagnosed with congestive heart failure and I gained ninety pounds of fluid due to increasing kidney failure. To my delight, the staff dietician was encouraging of my choice to remain an herbivore. She even worked with the staff to create some tasty meal options. Although the meals did not always agree with my gastrointestinal needs, at least the food options did not have parents.

The next person I met was my registered nurse. During my undergraduate studies at George Mason University, I met several nursing students pursuing their degree. I was impressed with how focused and intentional they were in their studies. They were always busy in the library or heading to a lab or practicum. Nursing students demonstrated a hustle that I certainly did not match as I pursued my bachelors of arts in history. Christine was cut from this same cloth.

As she leaned over the large secured medication cart, she managed to weave between engaging light banter and intent focus. Managed by her checklist, Christine reviewed the medications for each patient on Hall B as she prepared for her rounds. I came to learn that Christine, and not my doctors at Diamond Care, would determine the access to as well as the level and quality of my care. Christine administered medications, scheduled transportation to my outside appointments, communicated on my behalf with doctors, arranged for my clothes to be washed, and informed the custodial staff if I needed lotion, diapers, or butt wipes. We seem to expect way too much from the registered nurses at a skilled nursing facility. She performed all these tasks for each resident on Hall B and accomplished all this with a sweet disposition and efficiency. Her disarming nature even helped to lessen the intimidating presence of big God Emperor.

"I may not get stabbed, shot, killed or hurt while I am here," I thought. "Christine will look out for me!" As the internal clock in my head counted down my time left at Diamond Care, I realized that developing a relationship with Christine was key to my come back.

As solid as the medical staff at Diamond Care was, I realized that the key to returning to some normalcy rested on my interactions with the physical and occupational therapist staff. These medical wizards would teach me the techniques needed to have any appreciable quality of life. After my amputation, I had been exposed to a competent in-house therapy staff at a top rehab facility. They took me through the initial learnings of transferring from my bed to my chair, from my chair to my shower, and from my bedside commode to my chair and back into bed. Little tips like "Bend the foot on your good leg in the opposite direction of your transfer to gain better leverage," or "Slide to the end of your chair and bend over in an exaggerated manner to help you stand," are techniques that have served me well.

After initially being released, I was introduced to two therapists that came into my home. I was amazed at how they could take a household item and turn it into a workout tool. Occupational therapist could take a simple procedure like brushing your teeth or washing your face and make it a meaningful part of your recovery. Prior to my time at Diamond Care, I had been exposed to nearly a dozen physical and occupational therapists. For all the good intentions, I had spent the overwhelming majority of the past three months in bed, only able to sit up for a few hours a day during a stretch of that time. It was not their fault as we started out with solid goals, clear-cut goals, standing on one leg. Until I got fitted for my prosthesis, the measurement of my physical prowess was determined by my ability to stand on one leg and how long I could hold that stance.

"You should be able to stand up on that one good leg," one of the staff therapists said. With that proclamation, I leaned back in bed, and stamped my foot on the floor and tried to stand. *Bam!* I immediately went to the floor! Well, almost to floor as the therapist's knee broke my fall. With her small knee being the only thing preventing me from sprawling on the floor, I grabbed the assist bars and attempted to pull myself back to the safety of the bed. I did this while yelling, *"Help, help!"* at the top of my lungs until several members of the staff dragged me back on the bed.

Over the next couple of weeks, I could tell that falling spooked the staff and they became less aggressive in my treatment. Falling spooked me too, and, unfortunately lessened my resolve and diminished my progress. Falling became the boogeyman to me and the staff. And although no one wants to fall I had to learn to embrace it as part of the process. I came to see falling as a stern but necessary taskmaster, filled with data telling you what to do and what not to do. I later realized that I had to learn to face this monster to succeed.

I was determined that my time with the therapist staff at Diamond Care would have much better results. First, I would assess their level of competence, professionalism, and passion by telling them my health story…in detail. Not just the ills that had happened to me this year but also the fact that I had lost over two hundred pounds through a vegetarian diet. Without being obnoxious, I wanted to dispel any perceptions they may have had of me based on age, condition or any demographic that may cloud my care. Finally, I wanted to get the staff to match my sense of urgency as much as possible. My instincts told me that I was the youngest resident in this facility. Our shared mission needed to be returning me to my life as soon as possible, and not settling in for a long convalescence. I had many health issues and many adjustments to make; dialysis three times a week, five blood pressure medications, two diabetes medications, new heart medication, new gastrointestinal meds, a new, very restrictive diet, and it goes on and on and on. This therapist group, however, had one focus: help me to walk!

The eight therapists at Diamond Care were a tight-knit group. Housed in a little gym with dumbbells, mats, parallel bars, and medical equipment. This room was the lair where they provided techniques for steady, incremental physical improvement. This was by no means a state of the art facility, but it appeared to have everything needed to build back the energy and endurance that I had been robbed of by eight months of sitting in a wheelchair and being confined to a bed. They worked like a team of skilled ninjas disseminating their expertise in everything kinematic. It was all about strength and movement as each day, they would have me execute a workout routine that vacillated between arms and legs. I was amazed how much stronger you can become using small amounts of weights with high repetition. You could tell they enjoyed working with a younger and comparatively healthier patient. As they became more comfortable with me, they expressed that they normally worked with patients with less range of motion and energy. To increase their level of confidence in me, I constantly added more reps to my workout than they assigned. The highlight of each session was my walking routine. We began, cautiously, practicing standing and then sitting. Ten times, check! Then, with the help of a walker, we to took a lap or two around the small gym, check. During the next session, we walked halfway down the hall, check. Finally, we progressed down the entire length of the hall. The team was very cautious, wheeling a chair behind me while holding on to a belt tightly secured around my chest. While I do not believe that either precaution would actually break a fall, I acquiesced realizing that safety measures were necessary.

Everything was going well! I was feeling stronger on my feet and learning how to steady my balance. I was walking longer distances as well, walking through the dining hall down to the break area. The entire staff was very encouraging as they commented that I was much taller than they had realized. By the attention and praise lavished on me by the staff, you would have thought I was running a marathon and not walking a few hundred feet at a time. I had the staff record my walking routine and I sent the clip out to my family and friends. I was so pumped to share some positive news with people who had been praying for me during these past several months. Good news had been sparse. Good days were often followed by successive, multiple bad days.

It was true that I was still in a skilled nursing facility, away from my family, going to bed being serenaded by screaming patients, fearful of God Emperor, and having diarrhea every morning, but it did not matter as long as I had a chance to walk every day. During a prewalk check of my residual limb, the staff discovered a break in the skin on my stump. After two and a half weeks of walking, this small tear in my skin shut down my walking routine cold. The therapist was fearful that a tear may lead to a sore that could, in turn, become infected. Initially, I tried to talk them out of their assessment. When negotiating and charm did not work, I gave them the silent treatment coupled with icy cold stares. After a couple days of unsuccessfully campaigning to practice walking, I just got over it. I was not discouraged as my experience with the staff proved to me that I could walk and I was determined to continue to push forward!

A nursing home stay may not be comparable to hard time but it is certainly a lonely and isolating existence. During my incarceration, I had a few visitors stop by from time to time. Mostly friends from my church, my pastor, and a few of my fraternity brothers. The majority of my time, however, was spent alone either in treatment, in the dining hall, or being transported back and forth to dialysis treatment. The days started early, and although the food was not great, meal times broke up the monotony of the day. Thank God that I had my Mac to keep me up on events and connected to the outside world. Thanksgiving was coming, and Elaine and I decided to spend the day alone together. All day. I had not seen much of Elaine since I was admitted to Diamond Care. She was still unable to drive due to the seizures she started having the month before. The new medicine she was taking to prevent the seizures left her weak and rather irritable as well. Money was tight so we had to drip out the Uber rides to the facility.

In addition to all this, there was still a great deal of tension between Elaine and I as we were attempting to adjust to the changing dynamics in our relationship due to my illness. Prior to my recent health crisis, I had been the breadwinner, paying all the bills, and making 90 percent of the crucial family decisions. Elaine used to lavish praise on me and gratitude for giving her such a high quality of life. "You are responsible for *the life that we live.* Thank you." It was almost embarrassing, but I must admit I cherished that she felt that way about me as a provider. Now, due to my weakened state, Elaine became responsible for making a majority of the decisions for our family. As our savings dwindled, she became the primary provider. From April through October, she was also my primary care-giver. I was neither a willing or cooperative patient, to say the least. I attempted to do everything myself and strongly resisted any instruction about how to do things better. After one terse exchange, I felt so bad that I sent her and a girlfriend to a movie and a hotel stay for a night, just to give her a break from me! And though she had been a patient, loving partner, our interactions had become short and cold. She was sick, she was tired, and she was fearful for our future. This made me very anxious when I was around her as well.

The Break Room

When I was not in therapy or heading to dialysis, you could find me hanging out in the community room/cafeteria. Every day, I would wheel myself from the last room on the left into the front of the building and take my place in the back of the break room. It was quite a trip, but well worth the trouble as I perched myself into a position that both gave me privacy but allowed me to get a good look at all the happenings firsthand. I could tell that my constant presence at the preferred table upset the natural order of things as that table always filled first or second whenever I was late getting to the room. Days were long and lonely, but my time in the community room broke up the monotony.

It was quite a juxtaposition, me with my Mac and an iPhone sitting next to patients twenty years my senior in wheelchairs, bed-clothes, and hospital gowns. I also held court there as it was much more comfortable to entertain visitors there as opposed to my small residential room. The break room was the central network of the facility as well as several administrative offices were housed there and of course, the kitchen. I kept to myself as the residents participated in bingo, cheered as "Elvis" sung Christmas carols and watched OU play football on the communal flat-screen TV. Although there was limited socializing with the other patients, the staff had become my community; the dietician stopped by the table to see how meals were going, the therapists checked in between sessions, the administrators, cafeteria staff, and nurses said hi just to be kind. I would have gone mad if I had to be in my room all day as the break room was devoid of the smells and sounds of the rest of the facility. With old people,

Wi-Fi and a fresh pot of Folgers coffee, the break room experience was kind of like a Jurassic Starbucks.

Thanksgiving Day

Elaine arrived early on Thanksgiving Day. As we wheeled over to my favorite table in the break room, I reminded myself that Elaine needed and deserved my best today. She was still recovering from the effects of having two grand mal seizures but she looked beautiful. Wearing black slacks with her hair pulled back in a neat ponytail; her subtle manner still melted my heart. In her slight smile, I caught a glimpse of the way she used to feel about me. Elaine had brought with her several board games to help pass the time. Elaine loves board games as they reminded her of joyful moments during her teenage years in Maryland. I secretly hate board games as I find it hard for me to concentrate and focus on a competitive contest with no monetary reward. I needed, however, to get geeked up for this afternoon of playing. We needed easy time together as we tried to move forward in our new life.

"What game do you want to play?" Elaine asked.

"Phase 10," I eagerly replied as if I were actually excited to play. Fake it till you make it, I thought to myself.

Delighted by my reaction, Elaine and I settled into a multihour, intense session of the card game. With all my focus, I tried my best to administer an old-fashioned ass whoopin' in phase 10 that day, but Elaine pulled out the win in the end. She not only loved board games, she was very good at them as well! As Elaine waited for her Uber to take her back to our home, I was thankful that we had a day with lots of smiles and no tension. We laughed, we smiled, and even flirted a little. My lame jokes made her laugh again for the first time in months. For this, I was truly thankful and believed that our marriage might actually come out of this experience battered but stronger.

Dialysis

On Mondays, Wednesdays, and Fridays, I was transported from the skilled nursing facility to an outpatient dialysis clinic. From 3:00–7:30 p.m., three times a week, the catheter in my chest was hooked up to a machine that would simultaneously remove excess fluid from my heart and lungs while purifying my blood.

Your first trip to a Dialysis Clinic is like being inserted into one of those futuristic Tom Cruise movies. You know the ones where people are merged with bots to save the planet in a postapocalyptic world. The room is set up with twenty or so stations outfitted with a recliner beside a machine resembling a portable ATM, complete with a laptop connected to vials of blood and fluid. These five-foot-five bots are dutifully attended to by an army of masked medical technicians who patiently and expertly scurried between stations, checking vitals, adjusting fluid levels, and monitoring the constant changing flow of this life-sustaining process.

Of all the medical professionals I had met over the past year, the doctors, nurses and therapists, these gowned professionals meticulously grind through twelve-hour shifts, shuffling patients on and off theses weird machines. It was like being transported to another world.

What a racket, I thought to myself, as I thought about the money that ran through each of these blood transfusion terminals. This "racket," however, would save my life as it removed over ninety pounds of excess fluid I had gained as a result of my kidney failure. These visits would now be a part of a life-sustaining ritual at least until I could get a kidney transplant. Which would probably take years! The patients, nurses, and technicians there would now become part of my new community. For a younger person living in a skilled nursing facility, the thrice-weekly trips were almost a welcomed distraction, giving me some much needed social interaction in addition to critical care.

Another ball to juggle, I thought, *along with learning how to walk again.*

Kicked Out

On December 1st, the clock in my head that was counting down my time in the skilled nursing facility finally struck midnight. Without warning, two managers from the nursing home staff came to me after therapy and informed me that my insurance company stopped paying Diamond Care for my stay the day before. I no longer met the criteria necessary to certify my continued treatment. Mostly, the ability to pay!

Oh, I could stay but it would cost me roughly $250 a day depending on the services that I received. Since certification ran out the night before, they were giving me one more night to decide if I wanted to remain in their care. After this, they would need a credit card on file to pay the bill. Although jarring, I was prepared for this as insurance companies more than often determine the level and quality of care you receive and not your actual caregivers. In truth, if it was not for my nephrologist Dr. Neeravta advocating for me, I would not have even been admitted to a skilled nursing facility at all. She and my wife had made the critical call a month ago to proceed with an angioplasty and begin dialysis. As a result of that call, I regained some quality of life, and more importantly, some hope for my future. Before I started dialysis, I was bedridden with only the ability and energy to sit upright a few hours a day. Now I was actually walking! With that thought in mind, I gathered my belongings, waved the peace sign to God Emporer and the rest of the staff. As a buddy of mine wheeled me out to his Jeep, I stood up, and climbed into the vehicle. It was the brightest, warmest December day, steeped in hope, triumph, and possibility.

Three Months of Freedom

After Elaine was dismissed from her benefits coordinator position due to losing her license, she became a licensed insurance agent for an Oklahoma-based insurance company. Selling group benefits to local businesses, she thought, would give her the independence and financial freedom we needed to make our come back. After her initial training, I would be tasked with driving her around to her appointments until she completed her six months with no seizures. Although a good plan in theory, Elaine was never a big fan of my driving. I would also drive myself back and forth to dialysis three times a week. Elaine would ride with me and make sure I got in and out safely and Uber back home.

On day one, we got off to a rough start right out of the gate. With the assistance of the walker, I took my first step out of our new apartment and immediately fell to the ground. It is like my legs gave out on me as my foot got used to the new surface. As I laid on the ground, our new neighbors stopped by and offered their assistance. We turned down their help knowing that the fire department was on their way.

"What a way to introduce myself to the neighborhood," I thought. The paramedics watched closely as I made my way to the handicapped spot where my car was parked.

"Take your time, Mr. Lyons, we can help you any time you need help," they told me. I thanked them as I slid into the car. It had been several months since I had driven so we anticipated that I would be a little rusty. The last time I drove, I nearly wrecked my car in my wife's parking lot, getting my good foot stuck on the gas. We pulled

94

out of the parking spot and I immediately go through a roundabout. Coming to a screeching halt, Elaine looked terrified as we looked around to ensure no one saw us. I backed off the roundabout and proceeded to the main road. Elaine was furious as if I did this unlikely feat on purpose.

Sure, I crushed a curve or two, I thought. *Got to break a few eggs, to make an omelette,* I thought.

We avoided further incident during the five-mile trip to the dialysis center. Elaine got me inside and Ubered home. After dialysis, I would drive home. Elaine would meet me in the parking lot and help me get back into the apartment. This ritual lasted for two months as Elaine became more and more comfortable with my walking and driving.

Who Am I?

I once heard Darieth Chisolm say, "Who do I need to be to get through this." The victim of a domestic violence incident, she grappled with what she had to become to survive in her book *50 Shades of Silence*. Throughout my life, I had been many different personas.

Growing up, I was Little Darryl Lyons (my hometown folks were not big on pronouncing the N in my name.) Little Darryl was consumed with playing football, pleasing his parents, and going to church. He went to church every Sunday. He went to choir rehearsal every Wednesday. He sang in the choir. He memorized his resuscitations, he was obedient, obeying his elders, and he was dutiful. He would turn into "Big D," my stage name. At that time in my life, I was sure that I would be a singer/songwriter and "Big D" served as a great nickname with fellas and the girls.

In college, I was called "Genesis" the legendary founder of the Iota Alpha Chapter of Alpha Phi Alpha Fraternity, Inc. You would think that being the "Genesis" or the beginning would be a lot of pressure but not for me! I signed my first email as "DC Lyons" when I went to work for Synergy Corporation in Tampa, Florida. It was simply a shorter signature than spelling out my entire name. DC Lyons is an international businessman. He built a vendor program across seven partners, in five countries and ten cities. He created, negotiated contracts with foreign companies, he taught online classes, he is a blogger, he ran a Fin Tech start-up, he is recruited heavily, his opinion is highly thought of, and he develops people. He is thankful, prepared, and in the moment.

Elaine, the girls, and even my grandkids call me "Honey" which was short for "honey bunches of oats." This was something they all picked up on and gave me a great deal of pleasure. I often call myself, "The Korrior" which is my superhero name. It stands for "King/Warrior," which means I both fight and rule. To get through this, however, I would need to be someone I had not been before. Amputees have to think ten steps ahead, amputees have to be in the moment, and amputees have to have short memories. Men with one leg can't be afraid of falling, and men with one leg can't get ahead of themselves. Men with one leg have to keep an eye on the horizon while not looking away from the path in front of them too long. Amputees can't be bitter but they need to learn from the past.

Maybe I needed to be some combination of all the personas like in those superhero movies where, after a freak accident, the main character truly begins to know his or her own power and identity. All I know is that if I was going to get back any semblance of the life I enjoyed before my incident, I would have to turn into someone else.

Eight Worn-Out Tools

Be More Thankful

When I woke up from my surgery, my first thought was "be more thankful," or as some people say "be content." Prior to my surgery, I had never been "content" about anything. I always wanted more. To paraphrase an old Eddie Murphy joke, "If you gave me a rope, I wanted to be a cowboy!" There is nothing inherently wrong with wanting more. We are raised to want to surpass the accomplishments of our parents and their parents before them. But when that pursuit overshadows your ability to be thankful for what is in front of you, your perspective is misplaced. For years, I took so many people and situations for granted. I was not truly thankful. Sure, I said prayers and I was gracious, but I really thought my upbringing, education, or choices made me "deserve" the life I was living. I could not have been more wrong. Foolishly, I believed that good fortune was awarded to someone like me because I had a "special relationship with God" or because I am American. Now, after having everything stripped from me, I truly realize that "the rain falls on the just and the unjust," and we should rejoice every day we have breath. The day after my surgery, I received a call from a pastor concerned about my well-being. I will never forget what he said to me, "It is good to hear your voice, a lot of people want to be you today, you' re alive." Thankfulness is a worn-out tool.

Be More in the Moment

The book *Slipstream Time Hacking: How to Cheat Time, Live More, and Enhance Happiness* by Benjamin Hardy explores getting more out of your life not by adding time but adding experiences

> If we measured time as distance, on our death beds we could say, "It took me 80 years (or however long we lived) to get from point A (birth) to point B (the accumulation of a man's experiences)."

Life was best lived by slowing down and intently experiencing each moment. The best bosses I ever had, met with you for twenty to thirty minutes at a time, never looked at their phones, turned away from their computers, and focused on your every word. Because of their other responsibilities, they would carve out a short time for you and make you the "star of their show" for that short period of time. You felt refreshed and important, just because of the focus they gave you. How many of us live, give our direct reports, our children and our spouse the exact opposite experience, sitting at our desk, praying that time passes quickly, so that the clock turns 5:00 p.m. and we can go home. We sleepwalk aimlessly through the week, waiting for the weekend, or go through our weeks, mindlessly, not awaking until vacation. This numb zombie living serves no one as life passes quickly and we cover less distance from point A to point B. Think about how you would empower others if you gave them your full attention; breathing life into their thoughts and actions. You would be more fulfilled and they would be emblazoned not to do good things but accomplish great things. The next time your child asks you a question, turn toward them, take off your glasses, give them a big smile, look them in the eye, and say, "Yes, I am listening." Nod affirmations as they speak, mimic their gestures, and repeat what they said to prove that you were listening. I promise you that your conversation will be the most engaging and enriching that you have ever had. It will be the start of a wonderful, lifelong exchange. Being more "in the moment" is a worn-out tool, ready to use.

Be More Inquisitive

Inquisitiveness is the lifeblood of any lifelong learner. The smartest people are known to have great curiosity and they let that curiosity show in everything they do. They ask questions; drilling down to the essence of the subject or the issue. One of my mentors, Bill Quinn used to call this the "Five Whys." Do not stop asking why until you get to the root of the issue. What explains the exploits of Bill Gates, Mark Zuckerberg, Whoopi Goldberg, or any accomplished person but their desire to explore and learn more. At the height of my career, I traveled the world, and tried to learn about every culture I came in contact with. Travel can really whet your appetite about the world. And as I filled my passport I let my small-town upbringing drive my desire to see more of the world, wondering about the lives of the people I met, what they ate, what their home lives were like, and their purpose. Every plane trip to Asia and Central and South America was like a journey through the corners of my mind. Inquisitiveness is a worn-out tool.

Be More Prepared

When I was an assistant vice president at the Spirit of the Stagg Insurance, the best project managers were the ones who were most prepared. With back-to-back meetings ten hours a day, you had to prepare for meetings on your own time, the night before. I would have killed to find thirty minutes during the course of the day to prep for a meeting. It would have made a great deal of difference in the success I experienced there. As an entrepreneur, half the battle is preparation and the other half of the battle is follow-through. As an amputee, being prepared is more important than ever. Thinking through all the possible scenarios to get into your car, go into a store, or take a trip to the movies. Being prepared has now become a way of life! Never again can I leave the house mindlessly unprepared. Did I test my blood pressure? Did I test my blood sugar? Have I taken my meds? My health has forced me to prepare for each day in a way that I would have never imagined. Putting on my leg every day, getting dressed, and changing the shoe on the prosthetic leg. All a thought out process, in preparation for the day. I will take this worn-out tool into whatever professional environment that I go into.

Friends

During an illness, some friends really stick and some friends just don't. I was blown away with the love and support that I received from members of my family, my church, my fraternity brothers, and my former colleagues. Some people sent "love and light," and some people sent cash. You are going to be surprised at the friends that will show up and those who don't. When I think about my friends, I try to be understanding. Life often gets in the way of being the type of friend that we would like to be. I gave many people a pass during this time as I hope they gave me a pass during their crisis. Looking back, there were people I really showed up for during their crisis and people I missed during their lowest time. The frat brother with the life-threatening illness, the funeral of the gentleman that introduced my wife to me, the fiftieth birthday parties of people I grew up with. I convinced myself that I was too busy or it was too inconvenient to make time to attend. It really means that my "service light" was not on and this dulling of my service senses left me in a place where I could not offer help to others. I hope those people have given me a pass. When I was out of work, and before I got disability, I really leaned and depended on my network for work. One afternoon, I sent out 250 letters through LinkedIn offering my services as a consultant and training. I received a lot of sympathy, thoughts, and prayers but three people actually offered an opportunity to make some money. That's a good network as friends are worn-out tools!

Laughter

My brother set by my bedside the day after my surgery. During our conversation, I referred to my residual limb as "my stump." At that moment, my brother looked at my sister-in-law and began to laugh. He said that he knew when I said the word "stump" that I was going to have a sense of humor about this. He was right as I have found many instances to laugh at myself during my illness. I have been dropped several times all resulting in chaos and mayhem. The fact that you have to call paramedics every time I hit the ground is hilarious. The moment of panic before the fall is the best as you are not sure how to react in preparation for the fall. That moment is quick, awkward, and all-consuming.

My driving is a source of humor for Elaine and me, well mostly for me. Because of my prosthetic, I favored my left side when I am in the car. This caused me to hug the left line and makes for some uncomfortable trips for my wife. Plus, I have been known to "crush a curve or two" during our trips leading to her further frustration. One of my more sensitive moments during the first part of my illness is when my grandson, Ethan, first saw my prosthetic leg. My fear was that he would be scared of me and it would drive a wedge between us. This may have been my greatest fear as I prepared to see him for the first time. My wife and his mom told him that I was being rebuilt, much like Captain Dan in *Forrest Gump*. The only difference is that I had one mechanical leg and Captain Dan had two. This resonated with Ethan as we laughed and smiled at that thought. Laughter is a worn-out tool; use judiciously!

Faith

It is my hope that many of my nonreligious friends will find value in *With Worn-Out Tools*. Faith can be a touchy subject. "The evidence of things not seen" can be a heady concept for the noninitiated. The Bible says, "If you have the faith of a mustard seed, you can tell the mountain to be thou removed to the sea." The mustard seed is one of the smallest seeds of any plant. They are so small that many people will carry around a handful of mustard seeds as a physical manifestation of their faith. Although small, the mustard seed sprouts into a plant that defies its stature. There were days during my illness where my faith barely met the mustard seed requirement. I am not ashamed to say that there were days I doubted that God had a plan for me. When good days were met with multiple bad days, my faith was weakened and left bare. I am glad that God did not require faith the size of an avocado seed as I never would have made it. Faith is a worn-out tool.

Rule Number 1

That brings us to the most important thing that I have learned as an amputee. I call this "rule number 1," or "the mother of all rules." Your ability to apply rule number 1 will determine your success as an amputee. If you are an amputee, you must approach every task as if it is the most difficult thing that you have ever done! Every transfer, every slide, every shower, every stand up, and sit down. Everything you do requires and almost demands your maximum effort. Whenever you are challenged with any physical task, to successfully complete it, you will need to use your entire body to overcome it. It is just the rule as everything is an extreme challenge. I find myself having to be constantly reminded of rule number 1 as you can often be tricked into believing that some tasks do not rise to the level of requiring maximum effort. But this is just not true. As an amputee, anything you attempt to do for the rest of your life will ask for the strain and grind of your gut, your back, and your muscle. Beyond physical effort, any mental or spiritual accomplishment will require your maximum effort as well. Nothing any longer comes easy; nothing else is convenient. It is just the rule. The days of easy and convenient are over. When you are faced with any challenge that appears to difficult, refer back to rule number 1. This becomes your superpower as you now have the knowledge and the ability to approach everything you do with maximum effort. Imagine yourself as a student, as a worker, as a parent, or as a spouse, prepared to give maximum effort to anything you set your mind to do. The world is in no way prepared to meet someone with this type of singular focus. This type of flow. Rule number 1 is a worn-out tool.

One morning while I was putting body lotion on my right foot, Elaine looked at me and said, *"is that a wound on your good leg?"*

I want to thank every medical professional who assisted during my illness. The staff at Mercy Hospital and Mercy Rehab, My surgeon, Diesslhorst, my podiatrist Dr. Harkess, my PCP, Dr. Hopkins and the world's greatest nephrologist, Dr. Medipali and the staff at Oklahoma Kidney Care. Finally, I want to thank the team at Emerald Care.

About the Author

During a twenty-year career as a customer experience executive, Darren built relationships across the globe traveling to Asia and Central America over fifteen times and leading diverse organizations of over a thousand employees.

Darren and his lovely wife, Elaine, are based in Oklahoma City, and recently founded Korrior Inc. with a vision to create inspirational books and faith-based media projects. Recently, Darren became a trainer, teacher, and speaker with the John Maxwell Team.

He is available for speaking engagements at dclyons.ceokinc@gmail.com.

CPSIA information can be obtained
at www.ICGtesting.com
Printed in the USA
BVHW031447091121
621076BV00026B/301